10
minute
ecologist

books by John Janovy, Jr.

10

minute
ecologist

20 ANSWERED QUESTIONS
FOR BUSY PEOPLE FACING
ENVIRONMENTAL ISSUES

John Janovy, Jr.

St. Martin's Press
New York

A THOMAS DUNNE BOOK.
An imprint of St. Martin's Press.

DESIGN BY SONGHEE KIM

Library of Congress Cataloging-in-Publication Data
Janovy, John, Jr.
    10 minute ecologist : 20 answered questions for busy
  people facing environmental issues / John Janovy, Jr.— 1st ed.
        p.   cm.
      ISBN 0-312-17043-2
      1. Ecology—Popular works.   I. Title.
    QH541.13.J35   1997   97-13785
    577—dc21   CIP

First Edition: October 1997

10   9   8   7   6   5   4   3   2   1

CONTENTS

contents

ACKNOWLEDGMENTS

I WOULD LIKE TO THANK THE VARIOUS PEOPLE WHO helped with this book project. Scott and Elizabeth Snyder both read parts of the early manuscript and gave their comments and encouragement. Scott was a doctoral student in my lab at the time, and Liz was a middle-school science teacher in a rural Nebraska community. Some members of the Nebraska Nature Conservancy board of trustees also read the manuscript and provided comments. I greatly appreciate the education I received as a result of my service on that board of trustees, an education provided by the Nebraska Nature Conservancy staff, members of the board, and various individuals associated with the national organization of the Nature Conservancy. Cara Stanko and Kayleen Karnopp, students who worked in my office, helped with library research. Particular thanks are due Scott Slovic, director of the Center for Environmental Arts and Humanities—a remarkable program designed to help us articulate our relationships with the planet—at the University of Nevada/Reno, for supplying suggestions about additional readings.

I WAS SITTING IN A MEETING ONE DAY LISTENING TO ONE of the world's most distinguished scientists talk about biodiversity. His audience was made up mainly of business executives and attorneys who, because of various factors such as government regulation or marketplace events, suddenly found themselves dealing with environmental issues. As I looked around the room, I could see the audience paying close attention to the speaker. But afterward someone said to me: "I loved that speech but I still don't know what biodiversity really means or why it's so important." At that point I decided all these businessmen needed help. But they didn't have the time to go back to college and major in biology. That's when I decided to write this book.

10 Minute Ecologist was originally intended for business executives suddenly in need of education on environmental matters, whether because of government regulations, public protests, or even a feeling that maybe they should be doing "something for the environment." But it's also an excellent book for anyone newly involved in ecological issues, regardless of the nature of that involvement. My goal is to avoid polemics and provide plain, easily understood, nonthreatening information. I'm not taking a side in any debate. Nor do I believe this book is all a person needs in order to interpret the positions in a controversy. It will do wonders, however, for anyone who is now a CEO on his way to a public hearing on an environmental-impact statement but can't remember anything from tenth-grade biology. It will also do wonders for anyone who does not consider himself or herself a trained ecologist but who reads about environmental issues in the daily newspapers and asks, "Should I be worried about this?" My early manuscript readers were public school teachers; their favorable response to the "work in progress" suggests that *10 Minute Ecologist* may also find a useful place on teachers' bookshelves. Regardless of who ends up reading it, I hope this book actually serves as an introduction to the Suggested Readings on page 123.

I wrote this book as a series of relatively short answers to twenty questions. Each answer should take about ten minutes to read, thus the title. Nobody's going to become an ecologist in ten minutes a day, of course, but if we don't all make an effort to become more scientifically literate, then environmental issues will continue to be resolved in an atmosphere of public ignorance. There are not many secrets or big discoveries revealed in the following pages. Virtually all the information in this book is fairly common knowledge to professional ecologists. Many of the examples I've used have been written about time after time and cited in all the leading texts. But these questions are ones I've heard asked time and time again by responsible, concerned, well-educated, and successful people.

I've often felt that if paperback fiction, movies, and television all dealt with substantive ecological issues at the same level they deal with issues of politics, law, race, and economics, then maybe as a nation we'd be better educated on the way natural systems operate. As a result of this feeling, I've tried very hard to make reasonably complex ideas accessible to the same audience that reads paperbacks and watches television.

John Janovy, Jr.

10

minute
ecologist

1

how do we humans view the world?

HUMANS ARE LARGE, SHORTSIGHTED, VERY INTELLIGENT animals. This set of traits dictates how we view the world. Our worldview, in turn, often directs our actions. Actions, whether by humans or insects, always have an effect on an organism's immediate environment. At the very least, we all consume food and produce wastes, and many species, including our own, use natural materials to build "houses." We reproduce and increase in numbers, and we alter our environments in order to accomplish this reproduction. Other species influence our actions (disease-causing organisms, food- and fiber-producing organisms). The nonliving elements of our environment—for example, air temperature, water, minerals—also influence our actions. Organisms and their products are called biotic factors of the environment; nonliving elements are the abiotic factors. Ecology is the study of the interactions between organisms—for example, humans—and both the abiotic and biotic factors that influence their lives. But ecological interactions are dictated to a great extent by a species' genetic traits, and for humans, "genetic traits" means large size, shortsightedness, and intelligence.

Our large size is one of the most important of our traits, important in the sense that it strongly influences our interactions with other species. We see other large animals, and large plants, before we notice smaller ones, and typically we need to learn how to look for small organisms before we notice them at all. The smaller the plants and animals, the worse this problem of nonrecognition. But the vast majority of living things are tiny. The average size of animals is about half an inch long. Thus we are predisposed, by virtue of having been born human, to ignore most of the living creatures whose lives also depend on the only planet in the universe known to support life. This is the major problem most people must solve when trying to understand the natural world. Not only a ten-minute ecologist, but a ten-year ecologist, as well, must accept the fact that our view is distorted by our size, then learn to "see" the unseeable. Tiny worms occur by the millions in most lakes and many streams; bacteria cover the surface of every grain of sand; microscopic plants fill the oceans; fungi "eat" the beautiful fall leaves that finally end up on the forest floor.

Is all this little life important? Yes, it is very important. The richness of the soil, the ability of plants to trap nitrogen and make protein, and a host of other fundamental life processes depend on microscopic organisms. Most important of these processes is the movement of nitrogen through the environment. Without microscopic organisms, especially bacteria associated with plant roots, we would not be able to utilize the nitrogen in the air. Without nitrogen, we would not be able to build the proteins that are an essential part of our bodies. Without nitrogen, we would not be able to build the genetic information we pass on to our offspring. These statements are true for snakes and fish as well as for humans. In later chapters, the details of nutrient cycles and energy flow are discussed. But for now, we need only to remember that the flow of nutrients into our food, thence into our bodies, is ultimately dependent on microscopic life in the soil, water, and air.

Our shortsightedness is sometimes considered a trait that we inherited from our nonhuman ancestors. Indeed, shortsightedness is far and away the most common shared trait among animals. That is, virtually all species respond to immediate environmental changes (shifting light patterns, noises, passing members of the opposite sex, and so on) and tend to ignore the more "distant" factors, such as next year's price of corn and predicted oil shortages. We're not much different from the grasshoppers in this regard. Although certain individuals, and the insurance industry, try to plan far ahead, most of us spend most of our time worrying about, being happy about, and reacting to events that occur over a day or week.

Language and culture have given humans the power to act over great distances and relatively long periods of time, however. Furthermore, culture provides us with the power to act in large groups—for instance, nations and industries—to accomplish large tasks we could not do either as individuals or as families. Language and culture are as much a part of our basic biology as our shortsightedness. Thus we've inherited two opposing traits, one from our nonhuman ancestors (shortsightedness) and the other from our human ancestors (language and culture). One of these traits gives us the power to act over long distances and times; the other trait blinds us to the results of such acts.

"Environmental problems" are primarily human problems produced by the interaction between these two opposing traits. For example, because of our shortsightedness, we consume resources without worrying much about the long-term supply of them (water, fossil fuel). But because of our language and culture, we are disturbed by the thought of destroying the natural world, which many of us view as God's creation. Plants and animals, including entire species that may be displaced by our actions, don't worry about anything; they just live or die. Aside from possibly the apes, no other species has language and culture in anything approaching the human sense. So "environmental problems" have a very real philosophical component—namely, the question of how humans should interact with their environments, with the other species that occupy Earth, and with one another as individuals. But "environmental problems" also have a practical component, because Earth's ability to support human life depends to a certain extent on the planet's supply of nonhuman organisms, and on Earth's ability to sustain that supply.

Language and culture are products of our intelligence, and actions made possible by our intelligence are modified, in turn, by language and culture. Thus we also have a positive feedback system. Computers are a superb example of this feedback system at work. Mainly during the twentieth century, and primarily during the last half of that century, our intelligence gave us the power and inclination to think about ways to carry out certain calculations, and other mathematical procedures, faster and more accurately than could be done by people with pencils. The result of these language and culture activities (thinking and building) was the computer. The computer has, in turn, significantly modified our language and culture, providing new metaphors, new kinds of interactions between individuals and nations, new ways of waging war, and new sources of information.

The computer is only one of a great many human products that alter our vision and which are then themselves altered by that vision. Indeed, many, and possibly most, humans tend to view the world in terms of human products and through the vision-altering effects of these products. Human history is short, in the natural sense; a few thousand years is not a very long time. But during that few thousand years, we've been building things, modifying our language and culture, and consequently changing our view of the world because of what we've built. Some people claim that because of these feedback cycles, humans have lost touch with the planet that supports them. Other people claim that human activities are perfectly natural because we are, after all, a species of living organism that evolved on Earth. When these two groups of people get together, the result is often an environmental issue.

In the not-too-distant past, human products were primarily art, music, literature, machines, and buildings—relatively long-lived, tangible items. Recently, however, human products have come to include electronic images and sounds, which bear only a superficial resemblance to anything alive. These images and sounds can be manipulated in uncountable ways, and the results are often quite seductive for humans, who are, by definition, very intelligent animals who use their imaginations and often seek mental stimulation. We have thus generated a philosophical problem: whether our electronic images are "real." The answer is relatively simple: yes. Images are real. But (and this is a fairly large "but") these very real images, real in the philosophical sense, may have absolutely no connection with any of the natural processes that support life on Earth, and indeed may convince us that we've successfully separated ourselves from these processes.

Thus we've arrived at perhaps the most central issue of humanity's modern worldview, the question of whether our perceptions, upon which we so often act, match the reality of having been born large, shortsighted, intelligent, and ultimately dependent on processes carried out by bacteria. The answer to this question varies according to individuals, societies, and periods of history. The deeply religious among us may claim that the answer does not matter, for our lives are governed by forces over which we have no control, committed to ends we cannot fathom. The more cynical among us may claim that in an electronic age, we lack the capacity for joining our perception with the more earthly kinds of reality. Between these two extremes lies a vast territory of human thought, action, and rationale. Somewhere in that territory stands the ecologist, who believes that humans must act wisely in their relationships with Earth. And the more tightly human perception is governed by knowledge of the planet, claims the ecologist, the better the future looks for all of us.

2

what is a species?

A SPECIES IS A KIND OF PLANT, ANIMAL, FUNGUS, OR microbe. The word "species" is both singular and plural (a species, many species). Most people can distinguish a few common species— dog, cat, rose. Some people, particularly hunters and fishermen, can distinguish a few more species—quail, pheasant, mallard, pintail, walleye, bluegill, channel catfish. People who work in greenhouses and nurseries usually learn to distinguish several dozen species. People who frequent zoos learn some exotic ones—gorilla, hyena, zebra, crowned crane. In the overwhelming majority of cases, the species recognized by an average citizen are, like the citizen, large ones. Most people are quite surprised to learn that what they think of as one species may actually be several.

"What is a species?" is one of the most persistent questions in biology. People have been asking it for a very long time, and arguing about their answers for an equally long time. The question is persistent, and the answers open to discussion, because the criteria for distinguishing kinds are not always obvious. It's not too difficult to tell a zebra from a quail. But it's a little more of a challenge to learn to distinguish the three different species of zebras from one another, or the six or seven species of quail that live in the United States. In addition, remember, the vast majority of species are small, and belong to groups of plants and animals that we think of as exotic.

Small size and lack of information also contribute to our uncertainty about what constitutes a species among these relatively unknown organisms.

Most biologists use structural characteristics to distinguish species of organisms we call plants, animals, and fungi. Microbiologists may use some functional characteristics to distinguish between bacteria— for instance, the ability to grow in a certain kind of broth. Modern science has produced chemical methods for distinguishing between kinds—most notably the use of DNA (raw genetic information)— but it's still not clear how best to use such methods. In current discussions of ecology, especially if politics is involved, one often hears about "known species," "unknown species," and "endangered species." I'll deal with these subjects in a moment, but before I do, there are two additional things one needs to know about species. First, they are generally considered to be reproductively isolated from one another. That is, in the vast majority of cases, two different species either cannot or do not interbreed and produce fertile offspring. Second, the species is considered to be an evolving unit. In other words, species (reproductively isolated kinds) evolve from other species and eventually evolve into still other species. Species disappear from the face of the Earth, a process known as extinction. A species that dies out, down to the very last individual, has become extinct. So has a species that's evolved into another one.

"Known" species are better called "described" species. By "described," we mean that someone has taken the trouble to study the organism very carefully, decided which structures are best used to distinguish it from others, written a paper containing the results of such study, and published this paper in a scholarly publication so that other scientists have access to the information. In many instances, and ideally, specimens of the new species have been deposited in a museum. Thus if a scientist collects some organisms—say, ants—and wants to know what kind they are, then he or she consults the published scholarly works on ants, in order to learn how to identify the specimens, and may actually borrow museum specimens to use in accomplishing the task. For this reason, museum research collections are exceedingly valuable, and the expertise needed to maintain such collections helps dispel our ignorance about the natural world.

Attempts to identify specimens sometimes end in failure. You simply cannot always determine, from the scientific literature, what kind of organism you have in hand. At this point, you begin to suspect that you're looking at a new species that must be "described" as above. Then you do hundreds of measurements, make dozens of drawings, compare structures with those of known species, write the paper summarizing the results of all this work, and then submit the paper to a learned journal. Experts review the research, and if they find it acceptable, the paper gets published. You are then known in the discipline as the describer of a new species.

Described species must have scientific names assigned to them. Scientific names are much more than arcane professorly jargon; they are guides to the literature. Through use of a scientific name, a scientist can discover a massive amount of information about a species, because all of the scientific literature about that species also uses the same name. Sometimes scientific names are changed, because people do additional research and discover that the names need to be changed for a variety of reasons too involved to be included in this book. But someone skilled in the use of scientific names can trace these kinds of decisions backward in history to the original published description.

Scientific names of the hundreds of thousands of known plants, animals, fungi, and bacteria consist of two words: a genus name and a specific name. For example, the familiar pet dog is *Canis familiaris.* *Canis* is the generic name; *familiaris* is the specific name. This is the name given to the dog by Carl von Linné (Linnaeus), the man who invented this system of nomenclature in the 1700s. In print, scientific names are italicized. Sometimes species are named in honor of people—for example, *Salsuginus thalkeni,* a worm named after a landowner (Mr. Thalken) who gave scientists permission to use his property, or *Actinocephalus carrilynnae,* a species named after the describer's sister Carri Lynn. Species may also be named from some notable character they have, the place they were found, or other reasons. Usually the newly discovered species belongs to a known genus, and this fact dictates the generic name. If the species does not belong to a known genus, the scientist must describe a new genus, too, to go along with the new species, and make the case convincingly to the anonymous editorial reviewers.

Unknown species are those living in nature, unstudied, in many cases undiscovered, and certainly undescribed by scientists. Most people are very surprised to learn how common unknown species are. They are everywhere. We have a long way to go before we discover all the species that occupy this planet. The fact that most organisms are small means that a great many evade discovery. The fact that most organisms live in the tropics, where fieldwork is expensive and difficult, further contributes to their obscurity. In addition, human scientists are large animals that generally prefer to study large organisms, so tend to ignore the small ones. Unknown species are so common that almost any serious undergraduate biology student can discover and describe one, even in the United States and Europe, sometimes in a local meadow, especially if that student is willing to learn how to use a microscope well.

One of the central issues in the current environmental debate concerns biodiversity, a term that refers to numbers of species. The main reason biodiversity is an issue is this ease of finding unknown, by which I mean new, in the scientific sense, species. Thus scientists are able, by virtue of their knowledge about the number of unknown species they discover, to predict how many are yet to be discovered. From this kind of scientific activity, we know that our current inventory of known species, even though it numbers well over a million, is far from complete, and in fact may be but a small fraction of the kinds of organisms that actually occupy Earth with us. Scientists get uncomfortable in the presence of ignorance, especially when they can see decisions being made without sufficient knowledge to understand the consequences. This is the reason biodiversity is an environmental hot button.

"Endangered species" are those whose populations are low. Every species needs to be present on Earth in certain numbers to ensure survival. That is, the individuals must be able to find mates and produce offspring, or else the species will become extinct. A species needs a certain kind of habitat—for instance, prairie, marsh, mountaintop, desert—to live in. If the habitat begins to disappear, then the species does too, and if enough of the habitat disappears, then the species becomes extinct. Species' populations also need to be numerous enough to maintain genetic diversity through interbreeding. Although different species do not interbreed (in theory and usually in practice), individuals within a species (for example, your friends) vary genetically. When genetic variation is low, especially in small populations, then the species becomes susceptible to the effects of inbreeding—mainly, an increased frequency of genetic defects and increased susceptibility to disease. For this reason, major zoos screen their specimens genetically and try to exchange animals for breeding. As an aside, there are many species, typically microorganisms, that do not reproduce sexually. In these cases, reproductive isolation cannot be the philosophical basis for species distinction. Instead, such organisms exist on Earth as populations of clones. But we still often measure them, draw pictures of them, and describe them as species.

Although the current system we have for naming organisms is based primarily on the tenth edition, in 1758, of Linneaus's *Systema Naturae,* modern molecular methods have produced some interesting modifications of this system. Knowledge of DNA structure sometimes alters our perception of who's related to whom, and thus which species truly belong together in a group. Taxonomy is the science of classification; systematics is the science of classification as it is applied to questions of evolutionary relationships. Like all sciences, taxonomy and systematics change with new technology, including that developed by the molecular biologists.

Evolution is the unifying theme of biology. Knowledge about the species present on Earth is central to our study and application of this theme. Much of what humans do with their biological resources—including plants with medicinal properties, species domesticated for agricultural uses, and species harvested from natural populations—depends on our having an accurate inventory of life on Earth. This inventory includes knowledge of the kinds of organisms present, the places these organisms live, and the sizes of the populations supported by their habitats, and it is very far from being complete. In fact, there are many scientists who believe there are so many species on Earth that no matter how hard we try, with the available talent and interest, we will never complete the inventory.

3

what is biodiversity?

THE WORD "BIODIVERSITY" IS A CONJUGATE OF THE words "biological" and "diversity." "Biological" is an adjective that refers to life or life processes; "diversity" is a noun that means the state being diverse, or the condition of having different kinds of items. Because biological kinds are species, "biodiversity" therefore refers primarily to numbers of species. When a scientist uses the term "biodiversity," he or she is often talking about the tropics, where most of the world's species live. Humans are destroying the tropical forests at the rate of 50 to 100 acres a minute and have been for years. Because of what we know about the numbers of species in the tropics, this destruction means that we're also destroying most of the world's genetic information at the same rate we're destroying the forests. For this reason, biodiversity is an ecological issue among those who care about the world's supply of living organisms.

There are five general principles that a ten-minute ecologist needs to know about biodiversity. These are as follows:

1. Most of the world's species live in the tropics.
2. Prairies, wetlands, deserts, rocky coasts, and other identifiable habitats all have their characteristic fauna (animals) and flora (plants), as well as (insofar as we know)

characteristic soil microbes. Biodiversity for a Nebraska prairie does not mean the same thing as biodiversity for a rocky coastline in Mexico.

3. Most of the world's species live in and on other plants and animals—that is, they are "symbionts" ("sym" = together; "bio" = life)—a category that includes parasites.

4. Complex habitats support more species than do simple habitats (I've devoted two chapters to this principle, Chapter 10, "Why Are the Tropics so Complicated?" and Chapter 12, "Why Study Islands?"). ("Complex" in this context refers mainly to the numbers of plant species; habitats with high numbers are complex.) Complex places are usually varied in their physical attributes, as well as in the number of species they contain—for example, an island with mountains, valleys, waterfalls, floodplains, and lakes is a complex habitat. Such physical complexity almost always supports a relatively large variety of plants.

5. All of our present agricultural plants and animals were once wild, and biologists feel that the tropical forests in particular are filled with species whose economic potential has never been discovered or developed.

In order to talk meaningfully about biodiversity, a person also has to understand something of the taxonomic (classification) system used to classify plants and animals. This system is hierarchical—that is, it is built of increasingly inclusive groups, which are called taxa (pl.; the singular form is taxon). A genus (taxon)—for example, *Canis*— may contain several species. Canis familiaris is the dog, but C. lupus is the wolf and C. latrans is the coyote. So a genus includes at least one, and sometimes many, species, depending on the genus. Genera (plural of genus) are grouped into more inclusive taxa, namely families, containing at least one genus. Red foxes are similar to dogs, but not similar enough to be included in the same genus; the red fox *(Vulpes fulva)* is, however, in the same family as the dog (Canidae). Orders are still more inclusive, containing one or more families. Classes contain one or more orders. Phyla are very inclusive taxa, and all of the members of a phylum have a shared basic body plan. Thus our familiar dog belongs to the species Canis familiaris, the genus *Canis* (with wolves and coyotes), the family Canidae (with foxes and hyenas), the order Carnivora (with bears and skunks), the class Mammalia (with whales and humans), and the phylum Chordata (with fishes and frogs). Notice that in print, only the genus and specific names are italicized.

The more inclusive taxa (groups)—phyla, classes, orders—are often called the higher taxa. The less inclusive taxa—genera, species—are called the lower taxa. Habitats can be relatively diverse because they contain many higher taxa (orders and classes) or because they contain many lower taxa (genera, species), or because they contain both. A detailed description of the many known taxa and their geographic distribution is so voluminous that it now crowds the world's libraries. But as I said in Chapter 2, "What Is a Species?" the inventory of biological diversity still is far from complete.

When an ecologist uses the term "diverse," he or she usually means "relatively diverse," although the term "rich" is also commonly used. The opposite of diverse (rich) is impoverished. Some habitats are naturally impoverished (for example, small islands), while others are naturally rich (large islands with tropical forests, for instance). In theory, it is easier to preserve the diversity of an area by preserving the habitat than to focus on the welfare of one or a few endangered species. In practice, however, preservation of habitat does not always ensure preservation of all the species that live in that habitat unless it is of a certain size. In other words, a small marsh in the middle of a vast agricultural landscape does not support the same biodiversity as a large marsh. Again, this principle is explored in Chapter 12, "Why Study Islands?"

Ecologists have a number of formal ways to express biodiversity. These formal ways are mathematical equations that generate "diversity indices." In general, a diversity index takes into account not only the number of species in a habitat, but also the proportionate distribution of those species. A group of interacting species sharing a habitat is called a community. The diversity of a community depends on two properties: the number of species present, and the evenness in number of individuals per species. A community in which all the species are about equally represented numerically is more diverse than one in which they are not. For example, if one community has three species—A, B, and C—with 100, 120, and 132 individuals, respectively, then that community is more diverse than one with 175 As, 22 Bs, and 3 Cs. When the math is finished, the diversity index of the first community will be higher than that of the second, because the numbers of the species are closer to being equal.

But relatively equal numbers of individuals in each species is not always the natural condition. In fact, it is very unusual for numbers of individuals to be equal. So diversity of natural systems (prairies, deserts, rocky seashores) is limited in part by natural processes that dictate the numbers and distributions of organisms. Ecologists have been very interested in these processes for a long time and have devoted much energy to discovering and describing them. One of their more interesting findings is that in most cases, some disturbance of a habitat is necessary before that habitat will support the maximum number of species that could live there. For example, unless prairies burn periodically, their biodiversity will diminish with time. The death of large trees in a forest is another example of a disturbance that helps maintain biodiversity of the forest biota (plants, animals, fungi, microbes). Why is some disturbance necessary to maintain biodiversity? Because some species are evolutionarily adapted to disturbed areas.

A second, and perhaps more general reason why some disturbance is often necessary to maintain a high number of species is that disturbance produces what ecologists call heterogeneity. "Hetero-" means different. A heterogeneous environment is one in which there are different places to live. The more heterogeneous the environment, the more places to live, and the more species. In addition to their distinctive structural features (see Chapter 2, "What Is a Species?"), each species also has a fairly distinctive set of habitat (ecological) requirements. This set of requirements is called an ecological niche, and each species is said to occupy its unique ecological niche. Thus heterogeneous environments, with many places to live, also have many occupied niches, and consequently many species. Ecologists nowadays do not always agree on the best way to define, describe, interpret, and measure a species' ecological niche, and I've simplified this niche discussion somewhat, but it's not too far off base.

Scientists who are active in the conservation movement often deplore the "loss of biodiversity" due to human activities. These scientists are referring mostly to the clearing of natural habitats—such as prairies, wetlands, and forests—and conversion of these habitats into agricultural ones. A native prairie has many species of plants and animals; the cornfield made from that native prairie has only one species (the farmer hopes), namely *Zea mays* (corn). Routinely, even the cornfield has other species, such as insects and weeds, which cannot be killed individually in high enough numbers to prevent them from harming the corn crop, so these species are killed collectively with pesticides. In other natural habitats—for example, in the tropics—forests are burned, crops are grown for a few years on poor soils, and then cattle are run on the land. The results of these tropical activities are different from the cleared prairie in kind but not in principle. Conversion of "natural" areas to agriculture results in homogeneity (sameness) where there was once heterogeneity (difference). Thus we have loss of biodiversity. As long as there are increasingly large numbers of humans on Earth, natural habitats will be cleared for agriculture, so not surprisingly, the same scientists who deplore the loss of biodiversity typically also deplore the exponential growth of human populations.

There are both philosophical and practical reasons for worrying about the loss of global biodiversity. The philosophical reasons are explored in the last chapter ("Did God Make the Earth in Seven

Days?"); the practical reasons relate to the undiscovered medicinal properties and agricultural potential in the hundreds of thousands of organisms scientists have yet to study, and to the lessons to be learned about sustainable agriculture from research on natural habitats.

what is dirt?

DIRT—OR MORE PROPERLY, SOIL—IS AN EXCEEDINGLY complex mixture of organic (living, or derived from living) and inorganic (nonliving) materials. Furthermore, the nature of this mixture varies enormously, sometimes even over short distances. The structure and organic content of dirt determine, in part, the makeup of the plant community that grows in it naturally. The other major factors in determining the makeup of the plant community are temperature and moisture, both of which influence dirt, too, but often indirectly. The natural plant community in an area reveals the agricultural potential of that area. The combined effects of temperature and moisture, working over the long term to influence plant communities, are discussed in detail in Chapter 13, entitled "How Is Real Estate Really Divided Up?" Although we're talking about dirt in these few pages, the makeup of dirt depends on a number of complex interactions between other living and nonliving forces also discussed in later chapters. Because these interactions are so complex, ecology—ten minute or otherwise—is not easily divided into chapters. But dirt's pretty basic to an understanding of ecology.

The elementary property of dirt is its "particle-size distribution." Viewed under a microscope, dirt is seen to be made up of particles. These particles are what's left of mountains that have worn down from eons of being exposed to rain, freezing and thawing, blowing wind, running water, earthquakes, volcanoes, and rocks rubbing against other rocks, getting split by plant roots, and getting dissolved in acid. The particles eventually become dirt-sized and are transported, sometimes for great distances, mainly by wind and water. If the particles are relatively large, we call the dirt gravel. If the particles are very, very small, and all about the same size, we call the dirt clay. We have a lot of names for dirts with particle size in between gravel and clay. Some dirt is sand, some is loam, some is sandy loam, some is loess. The particles are not always all the same size, and they're certainly not all the same shape. The "particle-size distribution" is a listing of the various sizes of particles, and their relative proportions, in a dirt sample. Many of dirt's other properties—its ability to hold water, for example, and the kinds of plants and animals that live in soil water—are related to its particle-size distribution.

The second important property of dirt is its "chemical composition," which depends in part on the source of the particles (the source is called the parent rock, thus rock parents give rise to dirt offspring). If the particles came from rocks with a high iron oxide content (iron combined with oxygen), for example, the resulting dirt may be quite red, as in much of central Oklahoma. In fact, because of the chemical makeup of the parent rocks, dirt may have oxides of several elements, such as aluminum, silicon, calcium, potassium, sodium, and magnesium. The chemical makeup of dirt influences its properties. Clay particles, for example, in addition to being small, have iron or aluminum oxides. Particle distributions and chemical makeup of rock and dirt are very important to geologists, who can use their knowledge of dirt to figure out everything from the habitat of extinct animals to the behavior of murderers and their victims.

The third important property of dirt is its organic content—living organisms and their products that are found in the dirt. Soils are biological communities in the truest sense. Dirt contains a staggering diversity of organisms, and often equally staggering numbers of individuals. A partial, brief listing of soil dwellers includes bacteria, algae, fungi and their spores, amoebas, nematodes, earthworms, tardigrades, rotifers, mites, insects, rodents, tapeworm eggs, roots of surface vegetation, pollen, and seeds. Seeds buried but still alive, and able to germinate if given the chance, are said to be deposited in the "seed bank." Nature may draw on its deposits in the seed bank to repopulate exposed or disturbed dirt. A brief list of organic products includes bark, leaf pieces, cell-wall pieces, eggshells, hair, and dead bodies. A common organic component of dirt is feces. All animals, no matter how large or small, defecate regularly, and the overwhelming bulk of their feces ends up in the dirt (except with water-dwelling species, whose feces end up in the water). In fact, insect and worm feces are among the most frequently encountered biotic components of our environments.

Strange as it seems, some people like to eat dirt. Their dirt-eating habits get reported in the newspapers from time to time. It's not at all clear from these newspaper stories that purposeful dirt eaters know they're eating everything from tardigrades and rotifers to beetle and rat feces. Of course, a lot of us eat dirt accidentally, too, but accidental dirt is no different from purposeful dirt, at least in terms of what it contains. Tardigrades and rotifers are beautiful, mysterious, microscopic animals; they can't talk, at least in our language, but they probably don't appreciate getting eaten, purposefully or otherwise. Earthworms consume massive amounts of dirt. In fact, earthworms eat dirt and digest the organic materials from it, which is why areas with "rich, moist, organic soils" usually have a lot of earthworms. We don't know whether earthworms like tardigrades, rotifers, fungal spores, and rat feces; we do know that worms seem to thrive on such a diet.

Charles Darwin is a famous historical figure, mainly for his publication of the theory of evolution by natural selection in the middle 1800s. Amazingly enough, evolution is still a controversial subject, even though it has been established as a scientific fact. What most people don't know about Darwin, however, is that he published classic volumes on barnacles and earthworms. It's the unassuming earth-worm book, entitled *The Formation of Vegetable Mould Through the Action of Worms with Observations on Their Habits,* that concerns us here. Of course, there are astronomical numbers of worms on Earth. Darwin started, as he did with a number of other organisms, by keeping worms in the lab. There he studied their behavior and their mental powers. As a result of Darwin's worm studies, we know that earth-worms are prodigious consumers of organic materials and herculean dirt movers capable of burying large stones. He concluded from his studies that the entire surface of England had passed through worm intestines and would continue to do so forever. Then he extrapolated from England to the entire world.

Not to belabor the point, but Darwin was right. Earthworms are notorious for their dirt-moving—indeed, dirt-processing—capacities. One of the reasonably important ecological problems in the United States is the invasion of foreign worms. In many parts of this country, the native earthworms have been displaced completely by European worms, which have somewhat different habits and ecological requirements. There is no way to predict the outcome of this invasion, but the outcome is of more than curious interest to ecologists. Why? Because dirt quality and topsoil renewal are of major concern to agriculture, and the agricultural health of a nation is of major importance to everyone who buys groceries. Earthworms are one of the key ingredients, if not *the* key ingredient, in the production of topsoil. Good dirt—meaning dirt with lots of worms, of course—is crucial to the agricultural economies of nations. Agricultural economies tend to dictate all other facets of nations' well-being. Ecologists, even ten-minute ones, have little trouble equating the good life with a large supply of worm-turned dirt.

Dirt gets moved around by various factors in addition to worms, however—mainly wind, water, and larger animals. Some of these movements can be considered "local disturbances"—as, for example, when a gopher pushes up a mound of dirt in the middle of a golf course. Every time a tree falls over, the roots get jerked up, and this event produces a large hole of exposed dirt. One of the most general characteristics of life over most of the Earth's surface is that bare dirt doesn't stay bare for very long. To say that "vegetation covers the Earth" is to proclaim rather common knowledge. But vegetation *literally* covers the Earth (okay, there are a few bare spots). Seeds and spreading plants are common enough to convert most piles of bare dirt into weed patches in a hurry. The plants that first occupy dirt piles are often those with pioneer characteristics: small, easily transported seeds, relatively low water needs, relatively few roots, relatively large leaves in the seedling. Eventually, having been changed by the pioneer plants, the dirt pile begins to support more permanent kinds of plants, a process known as succession. Back to dirt.

Floods carry massive amounts of dirt, too, although these disturbances are often regional instead of just local. In 1993, for example, big floods throughout much of the Midwest deposited many inches, and in some cases several feet, of dirt and sand on what had been fertile "floodplain" farmland. Well, one of the reasons floodplains are fertile is that they get flooded every once in a while, and everything from tardigrades to tree branches to rat feces gets left behind with the soil particles. Then all the organic stuff rots, the earthworms move in, and in a few years the flood plain is covered with a rich, moist, organic soil. Then the farmers move in, too. Periodically floods return to floodplains, of course, but when the Missouri River dumps three feet of sand on your cornfield, you call it a disaster instead of a renewal. To the large, shortsighted human, the flood is a disaster; to the small, blind earthworm whose species has been here for several million years and likes rotten fungus and rat feces, the flood is a renewal.

Large-scale human activities often seem to start with digging in the dirt. Major construction (cities and highways), repairs (roads, sewers, and water mains), and of course agriculture begin with a bulldozer or a plow. In this sense we are tied tightly to our planet and must alter its very essence in order to make our homes and grow our food. In Chapter 19, "Do We Humans Live by the Same Rules as

Beetles?" I address this very question, and it's not likely to come as much of a surprise that the answer is yes. One of those rules is that like beetles—as well as gophers, termites, and a very long list of other organisms—we must move dirt in order to live, at least in our present state of civilization.

5

what is water?

WATER IS A CHEMICAL COMPOUND FORMED FROM TWO atoms of hydrogen and one atom of oxygen. The chemical formula for water is written as H_2O. Water is present, on Earth, and elsewhere in the universe, in a number of physical forms, ranging from gas to solid. Water is an excellent solvent—that is, many substances will dissolve in it. In fact, water has been called the universal solvent, because so many different molecules will dissolve in it. Beer, wine, and coffee with sugar are all examples of water containing dissolved substances. Water is capable of carrying not only particles of various kinds in suspension (as opposed to in solution) but also other liquids. Muddy water is an example of water carrying soil particles in suspension; if you put muddy water in a jar, the mud in suspension will usually settle to the bottom. Indeed, our own bodies are also prime examples of water carrying large amounts of dissolved and suspended substances, such as proteins, fats, carbohydrates, and nucleic acids.

The familiar physical forms of water are typically described as gas (water vapor), liquid (water), and solid (ice). But water exists on Earth in a wide variety of physical packages, and these forms have an impact on our lives. Not surprisingly, the various human languages have wonderful words for these water forms. Such words include clouds, rain, snow, glaciers, rivers, streams, bayous, lakes, seas, and oceans. These water words are often preceded by such modifiers as dark, torrential, blowing and drifting, alpine, rushing, meandering, lazy, man-made, stormy, and open. In fact, it would be reasonably easy for any teacher, from elementary school to university, to teach ten-minute ecology, as well as literature at the same time, simply by exploring our interactions with the aquatic world through these types of words and descriptive phrases. (I'm not sure we have so many colorful words for dirt, but we have quite a few for air.)

Naturally occurring water falls into three general categories: fresh, brackish, and salt. Freshwater is typically anything but fresh, containing as it often does bacteria, algae, uncountable insects, microscopic crustaceans, worms, dead toads, and duck feces. So-called freshwater does not, however, contain much salt. Salt water, as in the oceans, does contain salt, which is actually several different kinds of salts, including $NaCl$ (sodium chloride, or table salt), $CaCl_2$ (calcium chloride), $MgCl_2$ (magnesium chloride), and indeed some of virtually every chemical element present on Earth. Salt water also contains bacteria, algae, crustaceans, worms, dead fishes, whale feces, and an astronomical number of sperm and eggs. A lot of marine animals (those that live in the ocean) simply release their gametes into the sea. So when you go swimming in the ocean, depending on when and where this dip takes place, you're also swimming through a whole lot of sperm and eggs. Brackish water is diluted seawater, or partly salty water. Brackish water occurs along the coasts, where freshwater wetlands, rivers, and streams drain into the ocean and the freshwater mixes with seawater. A surprising number of plants and animals thrive in brackish water, and our coastal marshes are consequently rich, productive, and exciting places, biologically speaking.

In contrast to freshwater, seawater is remarkably constant throughout the world in terms of its chemical makeup. The ocean is relatively timeless and stable. The ocean is also very large, and so runoff from the small amount of land on Earth doesn't influence it a whole lot, except locally. Freshwater, however, occurs mainly in small amounts surrounded by relatively large pieces of land. This surrounding land varies enormously in terms of its geological history, its chemical makeup, and the way humans use it. Thus freshwater is extremely varied, according to its source, because of all the different kinds of stuff that drains into it every time the rain falls. Most humans get their drinking water from local sources, including wells and reservoirs. For this reason, we are, or at least we should be, somewhat aware of, if not concerned with, what actually drains into this water. As long as the stuff that gets in our natural water supplies is no more poisonous than duck feces, dead toads, and various microscopic wonders, then our treatment plants (and our stomachs) do a pretty good job of cleaning up our drinking water. But when agricultural chemicals drain off our nearby fields and contaminate wells, then we're in trouble and end up buying water in jugs filled up in presumably safe places like Maine, Arkansas, or Colorado.

To the average human, the movement of water is perhaps its most obvious and at times most dramatic property. Floods, torrential rains, hurricanes and typhoons, thundering surf—all are examples of water in motion. But the ten-minute ecologist needs to understand the phenomenon known as the water cycle. Any "cycle" is a process that "goes around"—that is, it occurs over and over again—with some of the same raw materials being used and same products being produced. In the case of water, what's here on Earth today is about what's always been here since the planet took on its present form about 4 billion years ago. Thus the Earth as a whole doesn't make and destroy water, it simply uses water over and over again, changing the form of this water in the process. So the water that participates in the water cycle is the same water that's been participating in this cycle for hundreds of millions of years.

"Water cycle" is a term that refers to the movement of water through and over the ground, through living organisms, into the air, and back again to the ground, where it again becomes available for use by organisms. One of the primary players in this cycle is the sun; solar energy supplies the heat that in turn stimulates the evaporation of water. Even if there were no living organisms on Earth, water would still move between the air and the land because of evaporation and subsequent precipitation, both governed by local temperature conditions. But Earth is pretty much covered with plants, which tend to lose water (a process called transpiration), mainly through pores (stomata) in their leaves. Many if not most plants have structural features, sometimes wonderfully complex, to help prevent water loss. But collectively they lose water anyway. Animals also breathe out water, and also have various adaptations to conserve it. But like plants, animals collectively lose water, too. So water moves directly from lakes, streams, ponds, and ditches into the air by way of evaporation, and water also moves into the air through the leaves of plants and the lungs of animals. Eventually, this water returns to the Earth and its living organisms as mist, rain, hail, sleet, and snow. When it comes back, we drink it, welcome it, curse it, or shovel it, depending on where it falls, when it falls, and in what amount it falls.

The present-day Earth has most of its land in the northern hemisphere and most of its water in the southern hemisphere, a fact that anyone can discern instantly simply by looking at a world map. Although land and water were not always distributed in this way (see Chapter 20, "Did God Make the Earth in Seven Days?"), the continents have been in their present positions long enough to have experienced several cycles of hot and cold climates. The cycles we know most about occurred during the Pleistocene epoch (Ice Age), the name geologists apply to about the last 3½ million years of the Earth's history. During the Pleistocene, the Earth experienced several periods of glaciation that we give names to, such as Nebraskan, Kansan, Illinoian, and Wisconsin (in Europe they're called the Günz, Mindel, Riss, and Würm periods, respectively). During these periods, vast amounts of water were frozen into glaciers that flowed southward well into what is now the United States, scouring the land and leaving stone rows known as moraines. During the so-called interglacial periods, one of which we're living in now, the Earth warmed, glaciers melted and retreated, and previously ice-covered land became covered instead with vegetation. Most of this vegetation, where the glaciers used to be, is evergreen forest (see Chapter 13, "How Is Real Estate Really Divided Up?"). The take-home lesson from both the water cycle and the Pleistocene is that cycles need not occur regularly at weekly, monthly, or even annual intervals. Cyclic events, particularly in the case of water, can occur continuously, as in the water cycle, or over several thousand-year cycles, as in the glacial periods, or, for that matter, on any time scale in between.

The interaction between humans and water has historically been of major cultural importance. Polynesian islanders became adept at using the ever-present oceans as a highway and a source of food, the Inuit made their houses of ice and relied heavily on blubber, ancient Egyptians dug canals, and today massive irrigation projects reveal our efforts to protect ourselves, and our economies, from the vagaries of water's natural movements. Throughout much of the Western United States, streams and rivers are dammed for flood control and irrigation. But the lakes thus formed are silting in at measurable rates, obvious evidence that even the tallest mountains eventually wash down into the sea.

The ocean, of course, has served as an avenue for exploration, war, and empire building, a source of literary inspiration, a combination grocery store and sewage plant, an arena for athletic endeavor, and a place to take a vacation. The ocean continues to be one of the world's last frontiers, and although our technology has become quite sophisticated, we still have a lot to learn about the ocean and the organisms that inhabit it. Because we're large, shortsighted, economically driven animals that are afraid of larger predators, we tend to view the ocean in terms of its commercial fisheries and its sharks and whales. A more proper view, however, might well focus on bacteria, algae, and diatoms. The tiniest organisms ultimately fuel the ocean food chains, which in turn support the increasingly larger species from squid to whales. As in the case of dirt, our understanding of water begins at the microscopic level, an assertion that might well be true not only of dirt and water, but of virtually all ecological phenomena.

6

what is air?

AIR IS A MIXTURE OF GASES. GAS IS TECHNICALLY A FLUID that not only has no shape, but also has the capacity to expand indefinitely. This air fluid (gas mixture) is in fact made up of molecules that are rather widely dispersed. Nearly 80 percent of these molecules are the chemical element nitrogen. About 21 percent of the gas in air is oxygen. The remaining part of air includes a very long list of gases: argon (about 1 percent), hydrogen, methane, helium, krypton, carbon dioxide, carbon monoxide, ozone, xenon, neon, nitrous oxide, water vapor, hydrogen sulfide, sulfur dioxide, and ammonia, to name just a few. The layers of gas that surround Earth are called, collectively, the atmosphere.

The amount of the various gases in air is influenced by the activities of organisms that live on Earth. It is common knowledge that oxygen is produced by green plants and consumed by animals, whereas carbon dioxide is produced by animals and consumed by green plants. But not all organism-produced atmospheric gases are so familiar to us as oxygen and carbon dioxide. Methane, for example, occurs in outer space and on other planets, but it is also produced on Earth by living organisms, in part through the breakdown of vegetation by bacteria. Termites are thought to contribute quite a bit of methane to the atmosphere, as are mammalian herbivores (such as cows) through their flatulence.

Other gases that occur in air, in part because of living organism activity, include thousands of kinds of molecules somebody or something perceives as an odor. Everything that smells is a gas, made of molecules that stimulate nerves in a particular way. The odors of perfumes, urine, feces, rotting garbage, petroleum products, and flowers, the rich smells of marshes, the piney-woods smell of northern evergreen forests, the characteristic odor of mildew, the aroma of yeast in a half cup of warm water, the unmistakable blast of dead skunk on the highway—all are produced by gases that make up air. In addition to perfume and sewage, there are many molecules that humans cannot smell but other organisms can, although "smell" may not be exactly the right word. Pheromones, for example, are molecules produced by animals that influence the behavior of other animals, typically members of the opposite sex. Although people may not be able to smell the pheromones produced by a female moth, the male moth can sure detect these molecules in air and usually flies toward their source.

Like any fluid, air can be hot or cold. Cold air is heavier than warm air, and when the two come into contact with each other, the mixing sometimes gets turbulent. When air gets warm, it expands, rises, or pushes on the cooler air around it. When air gets cold, it condenses, falls, spreads out, and pushes on the warm air around it. The air around the equator is, on the average, warmer, thus always lighter, than air in the more temperate zones. The air at the poles is, of course, always relatively cold, thus heavy. We use the terms "equatorial low" and "polar high" to describe these different air regions. On a large scale and in a grand cycle, the heavy cold polar air flows toward the equator, gets warmed, rises, then gets pushed back toward the poles. The Earth's atmosphere is in constant motion partly because of this warming and cooling of air, but also because of the planet's rotation. This rotation disturbs the large-scale air movements and causes wind to blow toward the equator predominantly from the northeast in the northern hemisphere and from the southeast in the southern hemisphere.

If you've watched old pirate or sailing-ship movies, or read the exciting books on which these movies are based, you may have heard the term "trade winds." Trade winds are the predominantly northeast or southeast winds produced by polar highs pushing themselves down into equatorial lows and at the same time being swirled by the Earth's rotation. The winds are called trade winds because they pushed and pulled sailers along their trade routes with predictable regularity. These winds also tend to disappear near the equator. When the trade winds stopped, sailing ships did, too, usually getting becalmed near the equator, far from land, food, and drinking water. Early sailors called these places the doldrums. We now use the term "doldrums" as a metaphor to describe a feeling of being stuck and feeling down and useless. As you can see from this discussion, ecologists, even ten-minute ones, are not above noting how human language is often enriched by our interactions with the natural world, including air.

Anyone who watches televised weather reports sees areas of high and low pressure spread across the continent and changing positions. In high-pressure areas the air is heavy; in low-pressure areas the air is light. We don't really understand all the underlying reasons why air is heavy or light at a particular place, but temperature has something to do with it. High pressure can be thought of as a pile of air that eventually collapses under its own weight and spreads out. Low pressure can be thought of as a sink into which surrounding air drains. Low pressure often portends interesting weather, because both warm and cool air can be sucked into a low-pressure area. Such mixing produces storms, which are bad for people who are afraid of lightning or getting hit by tornadoes, but good for people like artists, who like dramatic cloud formations. Blown-down trees and lightning-started fires are also natural phenomena that create disturbances. Such disturbances in turn generate temporary environments that some specialized plants require. Thus in an indirect way, for example, prior to the settlement of North America by Europeans, low-pressure areas had a direct influence on the native plant communities through lightning-started fires, which were ever-present although not always frequent.

In general, winds rotate clockwise in a high-pressure area in the northern hemisphere, but counterclockwise in a high-pressure area in the southern hemisphere. Exactly the opposite happens in low-pressure areas. These swirlings of high and low pressure are felt by all living organisms—plants, birds, insects, spiders, and bacteria, as well as humans. Many plants have seeds adapted to wind dispersal, the common dandelion being a prime example. Spiders are also notorious wind travelers; newly hatched spiders spin out long strands of web that are caught by the wind and carried great distances, usually with the baby spider still attached. For this reason, spiders tend to be among the first colonizers of areas stripped bare by fires, floods, and volcanic explosions. Of course, spiders are also carnivores, so unless some food insects also arrive, wind-sailing spiders tend to starve. But flying insects tend to get blown around, too, especially strong fliers such as dragonflies, and light but good fliers such as mosquitoes and houseflies. So the atmosphere can be thought of as an avenue of dispersal for many kinds of organisms.

Air also contains solid particles: dust, smoke, fungal spores, pollen, pieces of spiderweb, tiny flying insects, bacteria, to name just a few. "Dust" is a catchall word, of course, that includes as long a list of items as the list of those found in dirt. Dust is particularly interesting because of its colors (partly responsible for beautiful sunsets and sunrises) and because of what it can tell us about events happening far away, events that have already happened far away in time, and events that are likely to happen in the future. Scientists studying dust can determine whether a nuclear explosion has occurred, or a volcanic eruption, or erosion in an arid land somewhere. They can also tell us the kinds and weights of particles produced by various industries, warn us of particularly bad smog or allergy conditions, and predict the effects of wind on exposed ground. A ten-minute ecologist might be interested in looking at the famous Dust Bowl photographs from the 1930s; few sources of information other than those pictures can so quickly teach us about the power of air to move dirt and whatever else dirt contains.

Before closing this chapter, I need to mention both the ozone layer and greenhouse gases. Ozone is a molecule made from three oxygen atoms; there is a layer of ozone up in the atmosphere, about 12 miles above the ground. Along with all the other stuff in air—dust, clouds, and so forth—this ozone absorbs ultraviolet radiation from the sun. Ultraviolet radiation is generally lethal to living organisms and is one of the major contributors to skin cancer in humans, so this ozone layer is reasonably important to life on Earth. Certain industrial chemicals released on the ground move upward into the atmosphere where they interact with ozone and destroy it—in effect, destroying the shield that protects life from ultraviolet radiation. For this reason, most Americans can read as much about ozone in their daily newspapers as they can find in freshman biology texts.

Greenhouse gases are mainly carbon dioxide, which virtually every animal, including humans, breathes out regularly. Stove gas (methane)—which is also produced by termites, cow flatulence, and swamps—is another greenhouse gas, as are water vapor and various other industrial chemicals. Collectively these gases are called greenhouse gases because they absorb heat and radiate it back to Earth, thus creating an effect that operates like a global greenhouse. Under "natural" conditions, the amount of carbon dioxide in the atmosphere varies according to season in the northern hemisphere, where most of the land, thus most of the plants, is located. Plants use carbon dioxide, so the amount of this gas in air tends to be lower in summer than in winter. But clearing of forests and burning of coal and petroleum both increase the amounts of carbon dioxide in the atmosphere, thus increasing the amount of heat trapped and radiated back to Earth. In a doomsday scenario, this increased heat melts the polar ice caps and low-lying coastal areas will be flooded. Whatever the effects of human activities on global climate, the insurance companies who end up paying for hurricane and flood damage are, at this very moment, worrying mightily about the warming that may eventually cause massive coastal flooding.

Finally, air is a relatively hostile environment when viewed in terms of body fluids. Virtually all organisms tend to lose moisture in air, and during evolutionary history, colonization of land was always accompanied by acquisition of features that helped preserve body water. The hardened skin of reptiles, the waxy, hard exoskeleton of insects, and the kidney are all examples of such water-conserving features.

Dirt, water, and air—three general categories of nonliving components that make up our environment—are all seen to be complex and variable entities. Their qualities often dictate our relationships with them, and in this sense all are similar in their influences on our lives. We have the power to change those dirt, water, and air qualities, and we certainly exercise this power at least on a local scale. But we're all bathed constantly in air, which is always moving on a hemispherical, if not global scale. For this reason, air symbolizes perhaps better than any other environmental factor our shared dependence on planetary properties that may seem distant from our immediate daily concerns.

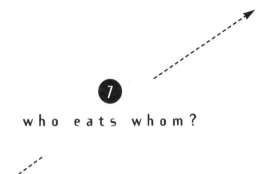

who eats whom?

A FEEDING RELATIONSHIP, IN WHICH ONE ORGANISM EATS another, is called a trophic relatioship. Thus a study of trophic relationships is a study of who's eating whom, under what circumstances, and in what amounts. The variety of feeding mechanisms and devices—among plants, fungi, animals, and microbes—is simply astounding, but basically, organisms obtain two things from their environments: energy and molecules. For most organisms, the energy itself is in the form of molecules ("Eat some sugar and get some energy!"). Although green plants get their energy directly from the sun, they use that energy to build molecules that contain energy; this process is called photosynthesis. The concept of energy being contained in molecules is one of the most central and important concepts in all of biology. Organisms need energy in order to build and maintain their bodies, just as you require energy, such as electricity, to build and maintain your house. Some molecules, in addition to containing energy, also serve as sources of building materials. What gets built from these materials? Cats get energy from mice, which they eat and then use to build more cat, for example. Cats also get energy from cat food bought at the store, of course, and use that cat food to build more cat.

In matters of eating one another, there are three categories of organisms: (1) producers, (2) consumers, and (3) decomposers. All the organisms we commonly call green plants are producers. Producers don't produce energy, they produce and store only an accessible *form* of energy. That *form* is a green plant. The form that energy appears in is vitally important to living organisms. For instance, if you wanted to toast a piece of bread and all the energy in your possession was in the form of sugar, you'd be out of luck. Similarly, sunlight, though a form of energy, cannot be used directly to satisfy your personal energy needs. Plants take the sunlight and convert it to a form of energy you *can* use. Conversely, most plants can't use electricity and gasoline, forms of energy that most of us use every day in reasonably large quantities because our technological achievements allow us to do so.

All the organisms we commonly call animals are consumers. Consumers eat organic materials—such as plants, other consumers, or parts of them. So in general, consumers eat producers. This feeding relationship creates a link between consumers and producers; not surprisingly, a series of such links is called a chain—specifically, a food chain. Seeds eaten by mice, which are in turn eaten by owls, constitute a food chain. Owls and other predators are usually rather opportunistic and will eat many kinds of animals. A dead owl, however, is often first consumed by its own intestinal bacteria, and then by insects, which become links in the food chain. But decomposers (bacteria and fungi) are pretty democratic; they'll eventually decompose both producers and consumers. Out in nature, all this eating and decomposing produces food chains that link many plants and animals together. An interconnected mess of food chains is called a food web, which is probably a more accurate metaphor than a chain to describe the trophic relationships between organisms in a natural environment.

Because we can view green plants in terms of the molecules they contain, green plants can also be called packages of carbohydrates, lipids, amino acids, and vitamins. Technically, these molecules are where the plant's energy is stored. The fact that you can burn a log illustrates the fact that a green plant is a form of (that is, contains) energy. The burning releases the energy. If you used the burning log to cook a hamburger, then some of that log's energy would have been used to alter the condition of the once raw hamburger.

Without green plants there would, of course, be no animals, at least of the familiar types; life, if it existed on Earth, would be quite different from what it is today. Because of the various properties of starlight (which is what sunlight is), it's worthwhile to speculate about whether life on other planets would include green somethings. Why is this speculation a legitimate one? Because the molecules that trap the starlight of the sun make the trappers look green to our eyes. Thus we expect that in a far-off galaxy, producers might well be as green as they are in your local cornfield or vacant lot.

Decomposers are the fungi and bacteria that break down dead producers and consumers into smaller and smaller parts, indeed back into molecule-sized particles. Decomposers typically secrete digestive enzymes (they "spit" on their food), which function to break up the food into molecule-sized bites; then the decomposers absorb the digested materials ("suck" it back up). The decomposers use these absorbed molecules to make more decomposers (bacteria reproduce by dividing; fungi grow and produce spores). Toadstools and mushrooms are the spore-producing parts of some fungi, so every time you see a toadstool, you're actually seeing part of an underground decomposer at work. And if you've had a tree removed from your yard, the ring of toadstools that appears regularly on the same spot is actually evidence that decomposers are at work, beneath the ground, getting rid of the stump and roots. Decomposing bacteria and fungi are extraordinarily common and widely distributed, and all organisms, even bacteria and fungi themselves, end up as decomposer food.

Consumers that consume green plants are usually called herbivores, or primary consumers. They're herbivores because they're eating "herbs," a term that refers mainly to nonwoody vegetation, although ecologists refer to animals that eat woody plants—trees and shrubs, for example—as herbivores, too. Herbivores also are called primary consumers because they're consuming producers. Consumers that eat herbivores are called carnivores ("meat" eaters), or secondary consumers. That is, secondary consumers eat primary consumers that in turn eat producers. The place in this food chain where an organism feeds is called a trophic level; in terms of feeding, producers live at the lowest trophic level and consumers live at higher trophic levels. It's important to remember that the energy in primary consumers was the energy stored in green plants, which in fact is part of the energy that fell on Earth as sunlight. This energy then moves up through several trophic levels because of consumer feeding.

It is a general rule that in nature, the mass (also called biomass) of producers is greater than the mass of primary consumers, and the mass of primary consumers is greater than that of the secondary consumers. In many cases, the *number* of producers (as well as the mass) is also greater than the number of primary consumers, and the number of primary consumers is greater than the number of secondary consumers. This decrease in mass and/or numbers of species as one moves up the food chain from producers to primary consumers to secondary consumers is often drawn as a pyramid made of stacked layers. The producer layer is widest, the primary consumer layer is less wide, and the secondary consumer layer is less wide still. You could obtain the same type of image by stacking a quarter (primary consumers) on a silver dollar (producers) and a penny (secondary consumers) on the quarter. Then you'd have a small pyramid. Logically, ecologists call this mass/number relationship between producers and various levels of consumers a food pyramid.

Food pyramids are conceptual and theoretical structures, just like food chains and webs. Their properties are observed in nature, however, in much more practical terms. For example, the grain necessary to build and maintain a mouse weighs more than the mouse; the mice necessary to build and maintain an owl weigh more, collectively, than the owl. But in order to discover this relationship between biomass and trophic level, we have to count all the mice that the owl eats in a lifetime. The grass necessary to build a zebra weighs more than the zebra; the zebras required to build a lion weigh more, collectively, than the lion. Anyone could discover this relationship simply by buying a kitten, weighing it regularly, and weighing the amount of cat food purchased to keep it alive throughout its lifetime. (Don't forget to estimate, and add in, the amount of energy the mother cat used to build the kitten before you got it.) There are also more seeds on Earth than there are mice; there are more mice on Earth than there are owls. There are more grass plants on Earth than there are zebras; there are more zebras than there are lions.

Why do these mass and number relationships generally hold? Because some, if not most, of the energy is "lost" when it is transformed from seed to mouse, from mouse to owl, or from zebra to lion. Where does the lost energy go? In very simple terms, it goes to keep the mouse, owl, zebra, and lion warm. That is, much of it is lost as heat. This loss of usable energy during transformation is a fundamental law of the universe, and we humans obey it as surely as seeds, mice, and owls. Thus coal can be transformed into electricity (coal-fired power plants), which can then be transformed into heat and electricity in your house. The coal was originally, many millions of years ago, plants, so it can be considered fossil sunlight energy. During the transformation of coal to electricity, some, indeed most, of the fossil sunlight energy is lost to us, and more is lost during the conversion of electricity into heat, such as that generated in a microwave oven or a clothes dryer.

Some animals are called top predators, because they eat other animals that in turn are said to live "high on the food pyramid." Often top predators are large, dramatic, sometimes exotic animals: Lions, cheetahs, and eagles are good examples. So are great blue herons, a common animal throughout much of North America. I've often thought that the great blue heron must be near the top of the food pyramid because it eats frogs. Imagine, for example, that this frog eats a dragonfly that's eaten a mosquito that's sucked a human's blood made from beefsteak, which is in turn made from grass, which originally got its energy from sunlight. In this food chain we have grass (1), cow (2), human (3), mosquito (4), dragonfly (5), frog (6), heron (7); the numbers in parenthesis represent the cumulative energy transformations necessary before the world sees great blue herons. I've always been surprised that there are so many herons in the world because they live, energetically speaking, so far away from the sun, even though they may nest in the tops of trees. But then herons eat a lot of small fishes, too, and the world's rivers and ponds are generally filled with small fishes.

When assessing who eats whom, one needs to consider what part of the world is being assessed. In other words, are we considering the tropical forests, the polar oceans, the grasslands, or some other type of habitat? One also needs to consider the scale at which we assess who eats whom. For example, in a roadside ditch, all of the producer, consumer, and decomposer relationships may be present, but on a microscopic scale. Conversely, out on the African veldt, seen so commonly on television nature shows, the producers and consumers may be quite large (but the decomposers are still generally pretty small). And out in the ocean, the food pyramid is mostly hidden from us. On the surface (both meanings intended), oceans seem to operate differently from terrestrial environments, but the seeming difference is due to the fact that most of us are not very familiar with oceanic producers and consumers. Much of the ocean production is carried out by diatoms, mostly microscopic, photosynthesizing, one-celled organisms that make beautiful silicon protective shells. Small shrimplike crustaceans, known collectively as krill, feed on these diatoms, and a large variety of consumers, ranging from whales to seabirds to squid, feed on krill.

All of this eating and decomposing results in the "movement" of energy and molecules from one organism, for example, a mouse, into another, such as a cat. Ecologists call such energy movement flow. Thus energy flows through an ecosystem (Chapter 9, "What Is an Ecosystem?") following the paths that are established by a food web. It's the molecules themselves—some of which are used to build plants, animals, and microbes—that actually do the flowing, and they carry the energy along with them. A cursory glance at the daily newspaper usually reveals at least one story about energy. Although the "energy" in these stories is usually electricity, oil, gasoline, or coal, all of it except the electricity that is produced by nuclear power was once sunlight trapped by green plants. Even hydroelectric power is ultimately dependent on the sun and atmosphere. For this reason, energy issues will remain in our newspapers, and in our political arenas, for a long, long time.

8

who beats whom?

CHARLES DARWIN BELIEVED THAT COMPETITION WAS THE driving force of evolution. Post-Darwinian scholars and politicians alike picked up on this idea, converting it, at times, into theories, such as social Darwinism, that today we find morally lacking. Competition, however, is an ingrained part of our society, and if the historical and archaeological records are correct, this has probably been true for several thousand years. But for ten-minute ecologists, competition needs to be defined in ways that go beyond athletics, war, and politics. We need to ask, and answer, questions such as: For what do organisms compete? How is this competition manifested? What are the outcomes of competition? We also need to ask a more fundamental question: Do organisms always compete with one another? This last question is easy to answer: no (or at least, probably not).

In any discussion of competition we need to agree upon the number of species involved. Competition between members of a single species is called intraspecific competition ("intra" = within). Competition between members of different species is called interspecific competition ("inter" = between). The average person who has not studied much biology typically thinks of interspecific competition when the subject of competition is raised. After all, on the athletic field Bears compete with Lions, and Eagles compete with Falcons. In nature, however, intraspecific competition (between different lions, for example, or between different bears) is most often the situation, simply because organisms of a single species are most likely to require the same resources. They're also likely to seek mates within the population of nearby members of their population. So here is a general rule about competition: *Usually we compete most strongly with those most like us.* This same general rule applies to all organisms, although not necessarily to competition for all resources.

There are two conditions that must hold before organisms can be considered to compete in the typical sense: (1) These organisms must use a common resource, and (2) that resource must be limited in some way. These are two of the essential conditions for "natural selection" as defined by Charles Darwin. Another essential condition is that members of a species vary in their ability to compete for the resource. When these three conditions hold, then "nature" is considered to "select" those variants that are most capable of winning in a competition for a resource. But "winning" does not always mean what the average person thinks it means. In this instance, "winning" means reproducing more than your competitors. The score is kept in numbers of surviving offspring. And to survive, in this sense, is to reproduce in turn.

Not all competition is between members of a single species, however. Sometimes several species compete for a limited resource. A good example of such a resource might be the flowers on a tropical plant. The organisms competing for the nectar from these flowers might include hummingbirds as well as several species of insects. Together, the species utilizing a common resource are called a guild. So the guild of species that rely on tropical flowers might well include hummingbirds and bees. Historically, the term "guild" also applied to a medieval group of people with similar interests and ways of earning a living— for example, shoemakers or brewers. From that usage, we have "guild hall" (union hall) and "guildsman" (member of an association of similar craftsmen). So it's not very difficult to see how the term might be extended to apply to a group of species that "work" on a common resource and assemble there. Nor is it difficult to imagine these guild species competing, much as medieval shoemakers must have competed for business in a particular town.

The average citizen, perhaps one who watches many nature shows on television, sometimes forms an impression that natural systems are always driven by competition. A ten-minute ecologist, however, should remember that not all resources are necessarily limited. Grass on a grassland, water in a tropical rainforest, and, some believe, food available to a tapeworm in a dog's intestine are examples of resources that are not necessarily limited. So one might ask: Did bison evolve their particular characteristics as a result of competition for grass on the Great Plains? The answer is probably no. Our best guess is that bison competed mostly for mates and developed certain of their physiological and behavioral traits in response to climatic conditions, but probably did not become such powerful bulls and skillful mothers by shoving one another aside to get at grass blades on the Great Plains where there was a *whole lot* of grass prior to settlement.

Competition for a limited resource may be quite subtle, and the long-term results of such competition are not always readily apparent. Plants may compete for sunlight even though sunlight is hardly limited. What is limited is the space and often the water needed so that plants can grow enough to get their leaves exposed to sunlight. When you "thin out" radish seedlings from a garden row, you're reducing intraspecific competition. Competition can be direct—picture a hummingbird feeding from a flower, thus preventing another hummingbird of the same species from getting the nectar from that same flower. Competition can also be indirect—such as a praying mantis that eats a fly, which then is not available for another praying mantis at another place or a later time. But in both examples, one organism is doing something that influences another's life—if not actually, then potentially. Sorting through all these forms, effects, and potentialities is often quite a difficult problem, usually involving uncooperative, and often not particularly smart or tractable, plants and animals.

Because of the great variety of organisms on Earth, the numerous resources for which they could compete, and the subtlety and indirectness of some interactions, the effects of competition on both the daily life of individuals and the evolutionary life of species have not always been easy to discover. So it's not surprising that ecologists have spent an enormous amount of time and energy studying competition. In general, as a result of all that study, here's what they've decided:

1. Competition is an ever-present and powerful influence on organisms' daily lives, as well as their lives as species. The competition can be for virtually anything an organism needs in order to survive, as long as the "anything" is in limited supply. But the outcomes of any natural competition are ultimately measured, and in fact summarized, in terms of offspring that in turn reproduce.

2. Organisms compete with all the "weapons" available to them. Such weapons include some familiar ones such as antlers, horns, and fangs, as well as some less familiar, or at least less "weaponlike," ones such as odor-causing chemicals, colors, behaviors, and responses to environmental conditions.

3. Competition between species may be mediated by the environment. In one of the most well-known examples studied, two species of barnacles competed for space on intertidal rocks, with the larger, faster-growing species usually winning. But on the higher rocks, the smaller, slower-growing species won, because it was more resistant to the drying effects of exposure.

4. Competition is still considered one of the causes of evolutionary diversification, although certainly not the only cause, and (according to some) perhaps not even the primary cause. Instead, "isolating mechanisms" such as chromosome differences that inhibit fertility are considered important factors in producing diversity among plants and animals. And, of course, mutations, spontaneous changes in the genetic material, whether it be DNA or chromosomes, are essential to evolutionary change.

5. Plants compete for water, soil minerals, and sunlight. Plants also compete with one another by releasing into the soil chemicals that inhibit the growth of other plants. And a whole lot of the competition among animals is for mates.

6. When you see some predator attacking prey—for example, a cheetah chasing an antelope on television— the predator and prey are not competing with each other. If the cheetah is competing in this instance, the competition is with other cheetahs, and the fastest one is most likely to catch the antelope. Conversely, the antelope is competing not with the cheetah, but with other antelope—again in terms of speed but this time speed of escape.

In summary, organisms do compete for a great many resources, but neither the form nor the results of this competition are always obvious to the average person. A ten-minute ecologist can easily train his or her eye to look for signs of competition. The best place to start looking is often in the backyard garden, and the first thing to look for is plants of the same kind placed too close to one another.

what is an ecosystem?

AN ECOSYSTEM IS A COMBINATION OF ALL THE BIOLOGICAL and physical properties of the natural world, usually in a recognizable area. If that definition sounds rather dauntingly academic, it's for two reasons: First, it *is* an academic definition, and second, the term "ecosystem" is not easy to define satisfactorily. Perhaps the best way to think of an ecosystem is to envision all the biological and physical events—plant growth, rain, temperature fluctuations, predation, parasitism, death, and so on—occurring in a relatively large geographic area tied together by some dominating physical feature. Thus one could envision, for example, "the prairie ecosystem," which would encompass a large, more or less self-sustaining, relatively flat and dry region in which perennial grasses were the dominant vegetation, characteristic native vertebrate animals were predominantly herbivores such as bison and rodents, and the major shaping physical forces were fire, wind, and extreme temperature fluctuations. If you're bored by prairie ecosystems, then of course you could envision a coral reef ecosystem, a desert ecosystem, or the most complicated ecosystem of all, the tropical forest ecosystem.

In the absence of human disturbance, ecosystems tend to remain stable for relatively long periods—thousands of years. During most of Earth's history, destruction of ecosystems resulted from global events, typically of geological origin, such as the drifting of continents and the rising and falling of ocean levels. The fossil record shows us that some, if not all, continents have experienced dramatic changes over the several hundred million years of their history. For example, America's prairie ecosystem "bread basket," the Great Plains, where most of our corn and wheat are grown, used to be a large sea. For this reason, enormous aquatic reptile fossils are found in places like Nebraska. In general, such changes occur slowly, or at least at a rate most humans would consider slow. It took well over a hundred million years for Kansas to change from a vast sea of salt water populated by swimming monsters (mosasaurs and plesiosaurs) to a vast sea of grass populated by walking and running monsters (mammoths and bison).

The concept of the ecosystem is a highly instructional tool with which humans may easily learn a great deal about their planet and significantly enrich their trips to museums and zoos. The concept is useful in this regard because it allows us to organize an enormous amount of information into manageable chunks. Much of this consists of information a well-informed person already knows but simply hasn't thought about in an organized, ecological way. For example, the word "Africa" is a fairly familiar one to us, and many African animals are also familiar, because we see them in a variety of places—zoos, museums, television, and *National Geographic.* In fact, we see some African animals—especially lions, leopards, cheetahs, zebras, elephants, rhinos, giraffes, and a dozen species of antelopes—so often in pictures that they tend to be a part of our stereotypical vision of the Dark Continent. The African continent, however, has many ecosystems— for example, the Sahara, the East African savannah, the steamy forests of the Congo River basin. Each tends to be characterized by its own mixture of temperature and moisture, as well as its own "food web," consisting of the species that live in those ecosystems and feed on one another.

In Chapter 13, "How Is Real Estate Really Divided Up?" I discuss the concept of a biome, which is a relatively large area characterized by reasonably stable vegetation types. A particular biome can occur anywhere, as long as the moisture, temperature, and soil conditions that produce it also occur. The term "ecosystem" includes and implies many of the same concepts as "biome," particularly stability and relative uniformity. But ecologists tend to use "ecosystem" in a more flexible way than they use "biome," and in fact the latter term is evolving somewhat out of vogue because we now know that pockets of certain vegetation types can occur within larger, relatively uniform plant communities. Such occurrence is dictated primarily by temperature, moisture, and soil type. In plain words, local conditions can alter the regional vegetation patterns (for example, golf courses in Arizona). Usually those local conditions have something to do with water, however—such as an oasis in the desert.

The ten-minute ecologist needs to be aware of two truly important concepts that apply to ecosystems: One of these concepts is that of "flow"; the other is that of the "cycle." Perhaps the best analogy for flow and cycling in ecosystems is the movement of money and goods through a society. Indeed, this analogy is so useful that professional ecologists share many ideas, methods, and metaphors with economists. Every time someone buys something, money flows and is transformed in the process. No matter whether the transaction is as simple as a child buying a piece of candy or as complex as a large real estate development, money flows and is transformed (from cash or credit into happiness and cavities in the instance of a child buying candy, to stress, livelihoods, construction accidents, insurance, and environmental hassles in the case of real estate development). Commerce provides an excellent model for energy flow and vice versa.

Societies also recycle items. Rumors and bad ideas are items that seem to move around fairly regularly throughout most societies, although in the case of these purely human constructions, movement is often so disorganized that it's difficult to tell where the cycle is. An obvious, and perhaps more serious, example of a cycle is the movement of the element aluminum. Most large cities have aluminum recycling opportunities, and if they don't have actual citizen efforts and pickup sites, then certainly they have can gleaners who dig through garbage to find aluminum worth money in the recycling market. Aluminum is mined from the ground, made into various things like cans and toys, then returns to either the ground in a landfill or back into the loop of useful, bought, used, then tossed (or recycled) products. Aluminum is also a good example to use in this context because it's a chemical element and chemical elements tend to move in cycles through natural ecosystems.

Energy, carbon, and nitrogen seem to be rather abstract concepts, however, compared with money and aluminum. Think of energy, carbon, and nitrogen cycles this way: People eat in order to get the energy necessary to work and play. Well, so do cats, rats, birds, and worms. Cats eat rats and birds eat worms, thus obtaining the energy to do the cat and bird equivalents of work and play. Rats, of course, eat almost anything, and worms eat dirt, thereby obtaining energy to do the rat and worm equivalents of work and play. When a cat eats a rat, however, energy flows from rat to cat. Some of the molecules in the rat—for example, those containing the chemical elements carbon, oxygen, and nitrogen—also move into the cat. When the cat defecates into the yard, or dies and is buried (with ceremony) in your garden, some of these chemicals, as well as some energy, get returned to the dirt. When the worm eats the dirt, the chemical elements and energy flow into the worm. When the bird eats the worm, some energy, nitrogen, carbon, and oxygen move into the bird. If the cat eats the bird, then the cycle is complete. The most important point for the ten-minute ecologist to remember, however, is that in all this eating, defecating, dying, and flowing, energy is gradually lost from the system, whereas the chemical elements are recycled.

The energy that is lost is replaced by the sun. That is, the sun's energy is captured by the ecosystem's green plants, then stored as plant tissue (leaves, fruit, bark, stems, roots), although some of this energy is lost in the storage process. But once the sun's energy is captured, it eventually becomes available to all those species that eat plants, and thus to those who eat plant eaters. Nevertheless, with each transformation, such as seeds into mice, some energy is lost (see Chapter 7, "Who Eats Whom?"). Where does the lost energy go? Into heat. An ecosystem can be thought of as all these life processes, involving the movement and exchange of energy and materials as described in other chapters of this book, all operating, linked together, and constrained by conditions of climate and geography. This integrated picture of life is what an ecologist understands when he or she hears words like "prairie," "desert," "coral reef," or "rainforest."

10

why are the tropics
so complicated?

THE TROPICS ARE COMPLICATED PRIMARILY BECAUSE THEY
have a large supply of both heat and moisture. Maybe, in order to be
scientifically correct, I should turn that statement around: Areas that
have relatively large supplies of both heat and moisture tend to be relatively complex environments. Thus when I use the term "tropics" in
this case, I'm referring mainly to the tropical forests, the steamy, exotic jungles of both fact and fiction. From an ecologist's point of view,
these types of habitats are clearly the most complex ones on Earth.
Why do heat and moisture make them complex? Major contributors
to this complexity are the multitude of different physical spaces provided by the luxuriant plant growth, the vast number of species found
in these spaces, and the many different kinds of relationships among
the organisms that live in Earth's warm regions between the Tropic of
Cancer and the Tropic of Capricorn (23° 27′ north and south latitude,
respectively). And the great range in elevation—from coastal wetlands to the high Andes—also produces varying conditions of temperature and moisture that in turn contribute to diversity of plants
and animals.

In areas with large supplies of both heat and moisture, plants grow

Information for the discussion in this chapter of tree density in the tropics is from
E. Pennisi (1994), "Tallying the Tropics: Seeing the Forest Through the Trees," *Science News* 145:362–66.

readily, a fact that's pretty obvious to anyone who's ever tried to grow a plant, whether it be a garden beanstalk or a philodendron cutting in the house. In the tropics, however, plant growth is so extensive, and there are so many different species, that the space over the land contains great variety in the shapes of organisms and their parts. To better understand the complexity of the tropics, we might first look at a typical mature tree in the United States. This tree has hundreds if not thousands of branches, all of different sizes and shapes and positions relative to the ground, and each branch has many leaves— hundreds or thousands in some pines, some spruce, and some of their relatives. The branches can be living or dead; dead branches can be broken off, exposing a jagged tip or sometimes a hole; part of the tree can be rotten, infected with a fungus, or attacked by insects—and each of these events adds to the difference between branches and between leaves, thus creating heterogeneity, or complexity. ("Hetero" is a word stem borrowed from Greek, and it means "different"—for example, "heterosexual" needs no explanation. "Heterogeneous" is an adjective that means "characterized by difference," that is, diverse; "heterogeneity" is a noun that means "the condition of being diverse.") The bark may be thick, providing many cracks and crevices for tiny insects and spiders. A woodpecker may have drilled a hole, lichens may be covering one side, or a fire may have scarred the trunk. And the roots, which are also quite varied, usually occupy more space beneath the ground than the stems, branches, and leaves do aboveground.

Anyone can discover this physical complexity just by studying closely the nearest tree, even the one in his or her own backyard. This simple bit of exploration, for which you pay nothing and will not be tested, is improved greatly by use of a magnifying glass. The trick to becoming a ten-minute ecologist is to learn to see this local and familiar plant as a heterogeneous mixture of spaces that can be occupied by animals, fungi, bacteria, viruses, and other plants. And, of course, the smaller the scale of vision, the more heterogeneous the world appears (thus the magnifying glass). That single tree in your backyard, by its very presence, with its various branches, leaves, and so on, produces heterogeneity—in your garden, in the space defined by your property lines, and in your life. So when we look at them closely, large plants even in temperate zones are seen to be quite complicated structures. In the tropics, this complexity is multiplied many times over, because there are so many plants and so many different kinds of plants. All this diversity and growth produces an astronomical number of ecological niches.

In ecological parlance, the word "niche" means a defined set of conditions under which a species exists (see Chapter 2, "What Is a Species?"). In a heterogeneous environment, there are many niches, thus many "places" for various species to live. Over evolutionary time (see Chapter 15, "How Long Is Short?—or, How Short Is Long?"), small organisms adapt to these niches, or in a more technical and abstract sense, create niches by living in them. One helpful analogy is the business office. Each organism's unique ecological niche is like an office, and the life history of an organism can be thought of as a kind of natural career. So the tropics, with their physical and botanical heterogeneity, provide jobs for vast numbers of tiny species—mainly insects, especially ants, and mites and spiders. The roles these organisms play in the ecosystem are analogous to jobs and have names like "producer," "consumer," "predator," "symbiont," and "parasite." When you watch a nature program on television, you're actually watching organisms doing something like trying to make a living at their particular jobs, using mostly only the genetic information they inherited, although the vertebrates may also be using information they learned on the job.

It's a general rule among organisms that each species has its own typical, and sometimes very specific, life history, in addition to its own unique structure. A frog that carries its tadpoles on its back, for instance, has a different life history from one that lays its eggs in the water, then hops off, never to mess with the offspring again. So with all those tropical species, we also observe equally diverse life histories. A species' life history helps define its relationships with its environment, too. For example, the tadpoles embedded in the parent frog's back skin have a different relationship with their environment than do those free in a puddle or in the water contained in a plant. So in the tropics we have not only physical heterogeneity produced by luxuriant plant growth, but biological heterogeneity produced by the many species, their many different life histories and relationships with their environments.

Life history differences are certainly characteristic of plants as well as animals. For example, in the tropical forests we find both rapidly growing trees, such as balsa, and slow-growing hardwoods, such as teak and mahogany, that are so prized for furniture, art, and utensils. We also find many plant species that have no roots, but live as epiphytes ("epi" = upon; "phyte" = plant) on other plants. Interactions between plants and animals also contribute significantly to diversity in the tropics. Fruit-eating birds, bats, and monkeys distribute the seeds that pass undigested through their digestive systems; beetles bury monkey dung containing seeds, thus increasing the chances of the seeds surviving a year; flowers and nectar-feeding pollinators coexist in a mutually beneficial, although mutually dependent, relationship; and ants evidently harvest a significant fraction of the wild seed crop. Some flowers are pollinated only by certain insects, bats, or hummingbirds; indeed, very dramatic evolutionary histories are often revealed by flower-pollinator relationships. And as might be expected in the forest, some plants live only in clearings created when large trees fall.

The number of plant species in a particular area of the tropics can be exceedingly high; in one study in Panama, for example, scientists actually marked 238,000 trees in an area about ⁶⁄₁₀ of a mile long and ³⁄₁₀ of a mile wide (a little over a hundred acres) and studied these trees for twelve years. The 300 tree species in that small area seems like a lot of diversity, but a similarly sized study area in Malaysia contained at least 800 species. A 1996 news report claimed that the record for concentrated diversity is in the Brazilian rainforest, where ecologists discovered 476 tree species in a 2.5-acre plot. American temperate forests, by comparison, are likely to have fewer than 20 species in a 2.5-acre plot.

Even a backyard ten-minute ecologist with access to a public li-

brary, a good bookstore, and a friendly commercial nursery could figure out the species diversity in a couple of neighborhood city blocks
and compare that diversity with the 300 to 800 tree species found by
the tropical forest biologists. My guess is that in the United States,
even the most upscale neighborhoods are rather impoverished when
viewed in terms of their botanical diversity. Similarly, or perhaps
partly because of the impoverished plant community, animal diversity
in most neighborhoods is very low. Suburban backyard animal diversity can be increased by keeping a rotting woodpile (I suggest sugar
maple for best results), planting flowers that attract insects, and set-
ting out a birdbath and bird feeders, but a year counting species from
your kitchen window will still reveal only a tiny fraction of the backyard biological diversity you'd find if you lived outside of Manaus in
equatorial Brazil.

Remember that a species represents a unique set of genetic information and that this information, taken collectively, is what spells
"Life on Earth" (see Chapter 2, "What Is a Species?"). About 70 percent of the Earth's genetic information resides in the tropics, or at least
did prior to the largely successful postwar wholesale destruction of the
rainforests. Most biologists who work in the tropics immediately face
a bewildering diversity of organisms, many of them nearly inaccessi-
ble to humans. In the latter category, for example, are the insects that
live in tree canopy high above the forest floor. Taxonomists—those
whose work focuses on the discovery, description, and classification of
species—tell us that there are about a quarter of a million known
species of beetles alone. Insect specialists who work in the tropics tell
us, based on the rate at which they discover new species, that there
may easily be a million species of beetles, and that they wouldn't be
surprised to eventually discover several million species of beetles,
given enough time and talent applied to the task. Of course, there is
not enough time or talent to deal with the beetles, let alone the
worms, flies, snails, and nematodes.

Tropical complexity is not limited to the forests. In the warmer
parts of the planet, we also find coral reefs, which are almost in the

same league as the tropical forests in terms of heterogeneity. Reef-building corals are members of the fascinating phylum known as the Cnidaria, which includes sea anemones, jellyfish, Portuguese men-of-war, and all their relatives. Coral reefs are characteristic of warm shallow seas, mainly because the animals that secrete the calcium carbonate reef skeleton derive much of their energy from one-celled algae living in their tissues. The algae live inside the coral animal's cells and carry out photosynthesis (see Chapter 7, "Who Eats Whom?"); the products of this process are then used for energy by the animal. The algae get a home; the corals get energy; the mutually beneficial relationship is known as "symbiosis" ("sym" = together; "biosis" = living). For this reason, fossil corals are indicative of ancient shallow warm seas. Reefs support a great diversity of fishes and of worms, sponges, crustaceans, snails, and other invertebrates, but like many if not most habitats, the animal life of coral reefs includes vast numbers of microscopic species. And, of course, even microscopic creatures have their own unique life histories and relationships with their environments.

Tropical deforestation is a global ecological issue for a number of reasons, one of which is the rate and extent of this human activity. People clear forests for agriculture and housing, period. During the last century, for example, the great pine forests of the upper American Midwest were cleared completely by loggers who thought the timber supply was inexhaustible. Nowadays, of course, we have bulldozers and chain saws, although in human hands fire—a factor that's been with us since the Earth was formed—also becomes forest-clearing technology. Population pressure and commerce increase the rate of deforestation. It's not at all obvious what the ultimate effects of tropical deforestation will be; predictions range from global climate change to political instability and economic collapse. If it's the latter, then repercussions will certainly be global whether they involve climate or not. Strange as it might seem, the molecular biologists are worried about tropical deforestation mainly because of the potential loss of genes that might in turn be the basis for new pharmaceuticals.

10 minute ecologist

For all these reasons, ten-year ecologists deplore the destruction of tropical forests and work hard to slow the process. Whatever the long-term effects, children being born this year are likely, within their lifetimes, to witness them.

why is the arctic
so fragile?

BY "FRAGILE" I MEAN EASILY DISRUPTED AND SLOW TO recover from a large disturbance. I gave this chapter its title mainly because of media attention paid to things like the *Exxon Valdez* oil spill in Prince William Sound and holes in the ozone layer. At the time of the *Exxon Valdez* incident, the newspapers were filled with dire predictions about the environmental consequences of not only the grounding and leak itself, but the entire Alaskan pipeline project. Pictures of oiled birds added to the image of destruction, and news videos of tedious beach cleaning supported the impression of serious damage to the ecosystem. Fishermen interviewed on television were angry and pessimistic about their futures. At the other end of the globe, ozone depletion ("the hole in the ozone layer") was at first most obvious in the high southern latitudes, and again, one read various predictions about everything from the negative effect on global fisheries to increases in skin cancer. I have no intention of trying to settle any such ecological issues, especially in this book. But the polar regions have served historically as a major source of natural products, while remaining quite foreign to most American readers, so a ten-minute ecologist needs some explanation of polar biology.

Virtually all ecosystems, including those at the ends of the Earth, are fairly resilient and tend to recover from natural disruptions such as fires, floods, earthquakes, and landslides. "Natural" in this instance means "caused by something other than human activity." The speed of such recovery varies, however, as does our perception of it, and as you might suspect, recovery time also depends on the nature and extent of the disturbance. In considering natural disasters, remember that fifty years is a fairly long time to modern humans. Indeed, people starve to death and die of exposure in a matter of days or weeks, and national economies can easily fail over five-year periods. But to the planet, fifty years is only an eye blink, if that, and a thousand years is not very long, either. So some terms that ecologists use—such as "easily disrupted" and "slow to recover"—are, like many other ecological descriptors, relative.

Biological processes are generally somewhat temperature dependent, and temperatures at the poles are low. In plain words, under cold conditions, like those maintained in your freezer, organic materials—such as leaves, bone, and skin—don't rot as quickly as they do in the tropics (think of the frozen mammoths that are periodically discovered in Siberia, or the frozen mummy of an Inca sacrificial victim, discovered after being dislodged from her resting place high in the Andes by a minor earthquake). When an ecologist says something doesn't rot, however, he or she is really saying decomposers such as fungi and bacteria that dispose of dead bodies and organic waste don't grow very fast or luxuriantly in the arctic. Other biological processes, however—for example, the growth of diatoms and the crustaceans that feed on them, as well as the breeding of birds and whales that eat the crustaceans—seem to operate at fairly high speed, in Earth terms, if left to their own devices. So it's not really correct to say the arctic is fragile because it's cold; but it is correct to say that on a human scale, the arctic often seems slow to recover from disturbance.

Before going much further, I need to point out again that the planet has two polar regions, the arctic (north) and the antarctic (south), a piece of rather common knowledge that, in an age of general geographical ignorance, no writer should take for granted. The arctic circle is located $66\frac{1}{2}°$ north latitude, and the antarctic circle is located $66\frac{1}{2}°$ south latitude, with the equator being at $0°$ latitude; thus the term "high latitudes" for the colder regions of Earth. Compared with the antarctic, the arctic is a veritable garden, primarily because the antarctic is dominated by the continent of Antarctica, whereas most of the northern polar region consists of ice overlying ocean. The water under the north pole retains far more heat than does the land under the south pole. Thus arctic summers are relatively mild, but "antarctic summer" is an oxymoron.

Strange as it might seem at first, in the summer daily temperatures fluctuate less at the north pole than farther south into Canada, mainly because the sun is above the horizon virtually all the time and there is little heat loss at "night." Similarly, in the winter, when the sun is constantly below the horizon, there is little daily temperature fluctuation because there is no daily source of heat. The antarctic is just plain cold; in the winter temperatures range from -40 to $-100°F$, although midsummer temperatures can warm to freezing ($32°F$). The history of polar exploration is really a history of human beings venturing into brutal environments that stretch our vision of ecological diversity on Earth.

Life at high latitudes includes some rather characteristic plant forms—for example, lichens, mosses, and stunted trees. Lichens are not really plants, however, even if they are included in some botany books, but instead double organisms—associations between algae and fungi. Lichens also grow slowly under the best of circumstances— so slowly, in fact, compared with the much more cooperative plants, such as rhubarb and begonias, that humans easily lose patience with trying to watch lichens grow, and conclude that they're dead. If you don't know what lichens look like, go outside to the nearest large tree; there's a fairly good chance some small ones are growing on old trunk bark. Take a magnifying glass along in order to appreciate the beauty of these lichens. The lichens in the arctic and antarctic, however, are ground dwellers and often much larger than the ones on your local tree trunk.

Moss can also be found in abundance in the arctic. True mosses, in contrast with all the kinds of things people often call moss, are mostly small plants that grow in clusters and as a rather continuous carpet, typically in moist areas. Mosses, and their relatives the liverworts and hornworts, lack the tissues known as xylem and phloem, which transport fluids within plants. Thus they don't have the kinds of internal structure that trees and shrubs have. The tundra ecosystem—flat, wet, and cold—dominates the far north (alpine tundra occurs at high elevations even at temperate latitudes). The permafrost line is about 60° north latitude; above that line the deeper soil never thaws, so water cannot drain down from the surface. There are nearly a thousand species of plants that live in the tundra, including fairly familiar ones, such as spruce and willow, that occur not as upright, stately trees but as stunted, even creeping, forms nevertheless recognizable to those who know what to look for in order to identify a plant species.

In the antarctic, about the only places for plants to grow are rocky, windswept ledges. This lack of space, coupled with the hostile environment and extensive ice cover, contribute to the rather low diversity of plant life in Antarctica, where about 400 kinds of lichens and fewer than a hundred kinds of mosses have been identified. Four hundred kinds of lichens seems like a lot of kinds to the average person, but on a global scale, 400 kinds of anything is not very many (remember there are 250,000 known kinds of beetles and almost 1,000 kinds of bats). The northern polar regions are much more hospitable to plant life than the southern, and the arctic flora includes a couple of thousand species of lichens, about 500 kinds of mosses, and nearly 1,000 kinds of flowering plants. But neither the arctic nor the antarctic are regions of high biodiversity compared with the tropics. Ecologists generally believe that stability is associated with diversity in natural systems. So the *relatively* low biodiversity of polar regions leads one to predict that the stability of these ecosystems might be easily disrupted.

On the other hand, the arctic oceans are, in many ways, highly productive environments. At the bottom of the food chain are algae—for example, diatoms, brownish or golden one-celled organisms ("golden algae") that are exceedingly common throughout the world and grow on the underside of arctic ice. In the arctic summer, diatoms become part of the suspension of algae that flourishes in the open ocean, especially at the surface. This mass of vegetation (an oceanic pasture!) is known collectively as phytoplankton, and it in turn supports large populations of small grazing animals—for example, small shrimplike crustaceans (krill) and other invertebrates, referred to, again collectively, as the zooplankton. Among the zooplankton one finds a diversity of small animals—for example, snails, jellyfish, comb jellies, and arrowworms—many no longer than your thumb, that eat mainly one another.

Zooplankton is the main food for baleen whales—for example, the bowheads, which can easily eat a ton of this shrimp salad a day by straining it out of the water. Fishes and squid also consume zooplankton, but then become prey to seabirds, seals, and porpoises. The polar food webs are thus characterized by massive populations of a relatively few types of organisms. Polar food webs also have some seemingly unlikely connections. In the antarctic, the blue whales, the world's largest living animals, weighing up to 150 tons, have as their primary prey 2-inch crustaceans (krill). A blue whale eats 3 tons of krill a day. One doesn't usually think of 150-ton blue whales, or even the smaller killer whales and penguins, as being particularly "fragile," in the commonly used sense of the word. But the generally low diversity of polar flora and fauna (plants and animals), compared with those of the tropics, these direct feeding connections between small and large organisms, and the large populations of consumers supported by standing crops of one-celled organisms and krill all conspire to make polar ecosystems fairly vulnerable to disruption.

For another example, global, and even cosmic, events that alter the amounts and qualities of light falling on the sun-starved poles can have profound effects on large standing crops of algae, thus on shrimp, fishes, penguins and other seabirds, seals, and whales. Such system-altering events range from volcanic eruption to sunspot cycles. Phenomena such as holes in the ozone layer and greenhouse gases, considered to be the products of human activity, can also alter the quality of light falling on the polar regions. This last observation is the basis for ten-minute ecologists' concern over the effects our daily activities have on the Earth's biota, and especially on the polar ecosystems.

From my personal encounters with many scientists over the past thirty-five years, it's my impression that the poles share one property with the deserts: the ability to simply capture the minds of people who go there to study nature. Of all the ecologists, geologists, and parasitologists I've known, those most wedded to the natural environments they study are those who've committed themselves to the study of desert and polar ecosystems. I have no idea why this connection should be so, or even whether my claim would be borne out by careful statistical analysis. But harsh environments have a way of reminding us that regardless of our tendency to place ourselves on a pedestal, we are, after all, just temporary visitors to one planet in a seemingly infinite universe. Scientists who study natural systems just seem to need that kind of reminder periodically, if for no other reason than to reinforce their values. This subject is dealt with in more detail in Chapter 17, entitled "Why Are Ecologists Such Nerds?"

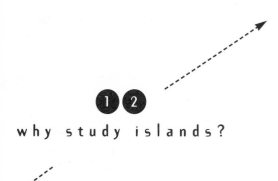

why study islands?

ECOLOGISTS STUDY ISLANDS FOR A NUMBER OF REASONS. First, many islands are beautiful and exotic places to work. Many are also miserable and isolated places to work, but working on them gets one away from telephones, committee meetings, babbling TV sets, cutesy e-mail messages, and annoying fax machines. Second, some islands bear special relationships to the nearest mainland, and for that reason are exceedingly interesting places biologically. Third, islands are sometimes "living laboratories," in that their fauna and flora are unique and relatively impoverished, and thus can tell us much about how organisms evolve in the presence or absence of forces that work on mainland relatives. Fourth, some of the best-known ecological research was done on islands, spawning a whole subdiscipline known as "island biogeography." Fifth, there are functional islands everywhere—that is, habitats that differ qualitatively from their surrounding environments. A good example of the latter kind of island would be a cattail marsh in the middle of a prairie. And finally, some of the theories about the space needs of plants and animals, developed during the study of island biogeography, are being applied to conservation problems in altered landscapes, providing us with answers to questions such as: How large must a wildlife refuge be in order to actually function as a wildlife refuge?

Perhaps a more fundamental reason for studying islands, however, is that much of the natural environment is distributed into patches of varying sizes—individual trees, lakes and ponds, fallen logs, the space under rocks, caves—and all of these kinds of places can, theoretically, be considered islands. Fish in a pond can't live in a nearby tree, for example, so the pond is really an island inhabited by fishes that are stuck in their "island." As is so often true in science, a study conceived as a fairly narrow one, designed to answer a basic question, turns out to have rather broad application. The work that spawned the body of theory called "island biogeography" was done by Robert MacArthur and E. O. Wilson on island species diversity. Like many important theories, this one has kept at least one generation of ecologists busy investigating its predictions and applying them to cases far beyond the islands that MacArthur and Wilson studied.

There are a few very important ideas about islands that have been revealed by research on them. One of the most important, and best-known, is called the area-diversity relationship. This idea can be expressed fairly simply as: *Large islands have more species on them than do small islands.* Ecologists studying islands, no matter whether the islands are glamorous and exotic ones (Trinidad, Tobago, the Florida Keys) or muddy, mundane ones (farm ponds in the prairies), always consider the numbers of species and the kinds of species, present as a basic part of the island's data. Large islands tend to be more complex and varied ecologically than small ones, because they have more space for different kinds of habitats to develop. A large island might have mountains, several different streams, forests, and coastal marshes, whereas a very small island generally does not have such a variety of habitats. This relationship between habitat complexity and diversity of life—namely, that complex habitats support relatively diverse plant and animal communities—is actually a fundamental principle of ecology. And this principle was developed most clearly by those studying islands.

Islands also differ in the rate at which they get colonized. The Galápagos Islands, Madagascar, and the Hawaiian Islands are examples of extraordinarily interesting islands, and research on them has greatly influenced our views of how islands get populated. How do islands get populated? By a variety of means, although the mix of immigrants depends on a number of factors, most important among them being a suite of properties we call vagility. "Vagile" means free to move about, but to an ecologist, vagility refers to those inherent traits of a species that provide motility in the geographic sense—over long distances. No matter how vagile a species may be, however, it still must cope with the distance between island and mainland, sometimes ocean currents, and prevailing winds.

Many birds, of course, are highly vagile because they can fly anywhere. Barn owls and barn swallows are so vagile, for example, that they occur naturally almost everywhere on Earth. Some spiders are also highly vagile because as microscopic newly hatched spiderlings, they spin out long strands of web that get caught by the wind and carried long distances. Aquatic insects such as whirligig beetles and backswimmers are also fairly vagile; in one memorable instance a backswimmer appeared one morning in a half-empty drink glass left on our deck after a party the night before. Cleaning up the morning after and finding a backswimmer in a glass on your back deck makes you think seriously about the various ways islands can be colonized. Freshwater fishes tend not to be as vagile as backswimmers, but humans have increased the vagility of many fishes by carrying them around in minnow buckets, releasing them, or introducing them into new islands of water as part of some "wildlife management" scheme.

Because islands are often difficult to colonize, the mix of species on islands is typically different from that of the nearest mainland, and the evolutionary forces acting on island species are therefore different from those acting on related species on the mainland.

One phenomenon that can occur when a species arrives on an island by happenstance is a sudden removal of the pressures of predation. Gigantism and flightlessness are two resulting phenomena that can arise in island fauna, in turn, when these pressures of predation are removed. Giant tortoises occur in a number of places in the world—the Galápagos, the Seychelles, and the Maldive Islands, for example. These islands are distantly separated, and the tortoises that originally colonized them were from different genetic stocks, so the gigantism evolved independently in the different locations. One finds flightless cormorants on the Galápagos Islands, but the best-known product of island isolation was the dodo, a giant pigeon. Large, slow, flightless, great-tasting animals tend to disappear when predators arrive on islands. In the case of the giant tortoises and the dodos, human sailors did the job. The dodo is extinct—killed mainly by sailors—and giant tortoises are uncommon. Sailors, including those aboard the *Beagle,* on which Darwin sailed around the world, took these tortoises along as food because they lived on ship and didn't require refrigeration. Lake Titicaca, high in the Andes Mountains, also functions like an island, evolutionarily speaking, and a flightless cormorant (a large fish-eating bird related to pelicans) has evolved there, too. Anyone who's watched cormorants knows that they don't fly much anyway, and are especially disinclined to fly when there are lots of fishes and other cormorants around, the weather's reasonably comfortable, and nobody's shooting at them. So the evolution of flightlessness in cormorants should not be too much of a surprise.

Lake Baikal, covering about 12,000 square miles in southern Siberia, is the world's deepest lake and also is one of the most isolated. Lake Baikal is another of the world's famous islands; it is filled with unique fishes that have evolved there, in a manner analogous to the evolution of unique life forms on the island continent of Australia. Lakes Titicaca and Baikal are aquatic islands in seas of land. The prairie mud holes mentioned earlier are just tiny versions of these famous lakes, but mud holes are rarely big enough, and don't last long enough, for unique species to evolve in them, and so tend to maintain their species diversity by drink-glass type immigration.

The theories of island biogeography are important in a practical sense, because they focus our attention on the areas and qualities of preserves and thus become an essential part of our resource management, and especially conservation, schemes. How big must a wildlife refuge be? is a question commonly asked by both politicians and conservation biologists (although perhaps for different reasons). The answer is: large enough to actually provide a refuge (if that's the intent). How large is "large enough"? That is a very good question, and its answer depends somewhat on the species involved. Whatever the species, however, the refuge must be large enough to dilute "edge effects." For example, a woodland designed as a refuge for birds that nest in the woods must be large enough to provide nesting sites far from the edge, to dampen the effects of nest predators and social parasites that naturally forage mostly along edges of clearings. A good example of a cruising social parasite is cowbirds, which lay their eggs in other birds' nests; small woodland birds such as warblers that nest near the edges of clearings end up rearing mainly baby cowbirds.

Thus "habitat fragmentation" is a major issue with conservationists, who see the breakup of habitats to be as serious a problem as the loss of habitats. In fact, breaking up a once-continuous habitat can be the equivalent of destroying it by, in essence, making "islands" out of a former "sea." Conversely, species that require islands, such as wetlands and potholes in a vast prairie, need enough of these kinds of islands to counteract the natural forces of drought, fire, and storms. Thus when the conservationists speak of trying to save a species, they're actually talking about trying to save enough of its habitat in whatever form—"island" or "sea," patchy or continuous—the species needs in order to survive.

1 3

how is real estate really divided up?

HUMANS TEND TO DIVIDE UP REAL ESTATE ACCORDING TO a bewildering array of reasons and methods. The reasons range from hatred and desire to tradition and necessity. At a minimum, the methods humans use to divide up real estate include contracts, inheritance, and warfare. In general, these human reasons and methods don't apply to natural systems (although it could be argued that a sort of necessity and a sort of warfare play major roles in the establishment of animal territories). Instead, in nature, real estate tends to be divided up according to available moisture, temperature, wind, elevation, latitude, geological history, and soil type. In other words, the abiotic (nonliving) forces that operate on the planet tend to be the primary factors that work to divide real estate into recognizable pieces.

These abiotic forces are not necessarily mutually exclusive. For example, elevation and latitude both influence temperature (the air gets colder the higher one goes up a mountain and the farther north or south one goes from the equator). Similarly, the soil type of a region depends at least somewhat on the geological history of that region. So in essence, when it comes to real estate, Mother Nature doesn't give a damn what humans think or want. All these forces of nature conspire to divide real estate into deserts, mountains, oceans, dry short-grass prairies, coniferous (evergreen) forests, tropical rainforests, deciduous (with trees that shed their leaves) woodlands, and numerous other types of places. Humans then come along and try to divide up the already divided real estate into nations, cities, farms, blocks, lots, and shopping malls.

But humans are not completely independent of natural forces. The agricultural economy of a particular region is dictated to a very large extent by the way Mother Nature divides up her real estate. The "agricultural" economy of the large coniferous forests is almost always timber and furs. Similarly, the agricultural economy of those areas Mother Nature has set aside as grasslands is most likely to be grain and domestic stock production. This principle—natural phenomena dictate agricultural economy—is not very difficult to understand. Prior to the discovery of mineral wealth (oil, coal, gold) in various places, the inhabitants of a region typically lived according to the prevailing agricultural economy. Often social structures and literature—religion, family rituals, entertainment, education, myths, songs, and stories—were, and to a great extent still are, strongly influenced by Mother Nature's real estate transactions.

But mineral wealth—an accident of geological history—completely alters the overall economic picture, as, for example, in the Middle East, where oil has temporarily changed a predominantly desert agricultural economy into an economy based on the global price and supply of fossil fuel. In the process, the political importance of various Middle Eastern nations has been altered significantly because of the modern relationship between petroleum, no matter where it comes from, and social-political events—including war, because nations (human structures superimposed on natural real estate) that rely heavily on petroleum are likely to fight to keep their supplies. But without modern technology and mineral wealth accidents, economies are still tied mostly to Mother Nature's real estate transactions.

The word "biome" is commonly used to describe the various kinds of natural divisions in real estate—it refers to any one of several major kinds of ecological communities, dominated by certain plant types. One hears of the "desert biome," the "alpine tundra biome," the "tropical rainforest biome," etc. The term "biome" is a useful one, because it combines an enormous amount of information into a small phrase or pair of words, then allows even a ten-minute ecologist to communicate that wealth of information. Why is this true? Because specific biomes—for example, prairie, savannah, or deciduous forest—are established on the basis of their dominant vegetation, which in turn is a reflection of the available moisture and temperature. The natural vegetation of a particular biome, the vegetation that dictates agricultural economies, is called the climax vegetation. Climax vegetation is the tallest, most water-demanding vegetation that can grow in a particular area, given the long-term supply of water and temperature.

Among the most classic of all ecological research is that done on "succession," or the sequence of plants and animals that occupy a disturbed area. For example, a plowed field is a disturbance, and the images we have of heroic pioneers and settlers clearing the land and putting in crops are actually mental pictures of people stripping off the climax vegetation that characterized a relatively stable biome. What happens when a cultivated field is abandoned? Virtually everyone knows the answer to that question: The field is repopulated by weeds, which give way to more long-lived plants, and eventually the field returns to a state so close to its original one that only experts can tell that there was ever a plowed field on that site.

What enables the experts to determine this bit of history? The experts we're talking about are actually plant specialists who can "read" the vegetation and recover the land-use history from the mix of species and the ages of individual plants. The repopulation sequence—beginning with "weeds" and ending with longer-lived plants—is called succession because generally one type of vegetation succeeds another. "Weeds" are weeds primarily because they intrude into our lives whenever we decide to start a succession sequence, for example by digging up a plot for an intended garden. Weeds can also be thought of as hardy and opportunistic pioneers, a more flattering viewpoint than, well, *weeds.*

Succession proceeds at different rates and to different ends, depending on the region of the planet where it occurs. Those rates and ends are largely a product of available moisture and temperature.

There are some fairly famous pictures in the ecological literature. One is of a triangle graph that looks something like a mountain, with moisture content increasing from left to right across the bottom, and temperature decreasing from hot to cold as one ascends from the bottom to the top. Obviously, each point on this triangle is a unique combination of temperature and moisture. In this iconographic mountain graph picture, various regions are labeled with their climax-vegetation type according to these temperature and moisture combinations. I have always thought this to be a pretty instructive picture, explaining, in relatively simple terms, the origin of deserts, deciduous forests, and tundras.

The other famous picture shows two views of the changing vegetation of North America, especially the United States and Canada, as one travels from east to west at a single latitude, and south to north at a single longitude. The east-west drive is at about the latitude of Interstate 40 (from the Carolinas to Bakersfield, California, roughly along the 36th parallel). The changing vegetation one sees on this trip is more a reflection of decreasing moisture than of different temperatures (because I-40 is about the same distance from the equator along most of its transcontinental length). At Raleigh, North Carolina, with average (Fahrenheit) temperatures ranging from the 50s in winter to the high 80s in summer, and 45 to 50 inches of precipitation a year, including about ten days of rain or snow a month, the climax vegetation is mixed deciduous and pine forest (the textbooks call it temperate deciduous forest). At Bakersfield, California, winter high temperatures are also generally in the 50s, and summer highs are in the 90s, but that city experiences only about three days of rain a month, and a total of only 8 to 16 inches of precipitation a year. Not surprisingly, the textbooks call Bakersfield a desert.

There are no interstate highways that are laid out along the 100th meridian, so a ten-minute ecologist wishing to experience the other half of this famous picture would have to wend his or her way northward along blue highways from western Oklahoma to Manitoba (where the roads pretty much end a hundred miles north of Winnipeg). In places like Kingfisher, Oklahoma, highs range from the high 40s in winter to the mid-90s in summer, with about six days a month and 25 inches a year of precipitation. At La Pas, the "jumping-off place" for the great northern Manitoba wilderness, January highs are near 0 degrees Fahrenheit, and July highs are in the 70s, with almost nine days a month and 15 to 20 inches a year of precipitation. Climax vegetation at Kingfisher is perennial grass ("mixed and short-grass prairie"); at La Pas, one steps out of town into the boreal, or northern, coniferous forest, which pretty much circles the globe at the higher northern latitudes.

Current thinking about climax vegetation is that it may be more localized than once thought, so that within a region, there will be pockets of seemingly out-of-place vegetation. For instance, on the Great Plains, although the dominant vegetation may be perennial grasses, there will be places where trees take over naturally. There are also places where trees take over unnaturally—as in landscaped yards where exotics are watered regularly. There are these pockets of seemingly out-of-place vegetation types throughout much of the world, so that when one looks at a vegetation map, one sees a complex patchwork at small scales. But superimposed on that patchwork are the larger patterns of the climax vegetation.

Real estate is also divided up into continents, subcontinents, peninsulas, and islands. And if we consider bodies of water "real estate," we have to then add streams, rivers, ponds, lakes, roadside ditches, rain puddles, fjords, bays, and oceans. In other words, natural physical spaces created by the distribution of land and water are as highly diverse in size and kind as are the legal spaces created by contracts and deeds. Humans tend to dictate the activities conducted in their spaces, but then humans also create legal spaces for the express purpose of dictating the activities; examples of this latter principle are artists' studios and church sanctuaries. The structure and location of natural physical spaces, however, have a profound effect on the spaces' occupants and their activities.

Ten-minute ecologists are constantly aware of their surroundings and tend to interpret their observations in terms of their knowledge of nature. But awareness is the cheapest of all traits to acquire—*much* less expensive than a college education. Ten-minute ecologists can very easily acquire a significant measure of awareness simply by browsing through an atlas prior to travel, reading about natural vegetation in places where they and their relatives live, and taking advantage of botanical gardens when they're available. But be forewarned. Awareness of the natural world has a tendency to turn normal people into eco-tourists (which some of us believe is not all that much of a disaster).

1 4

how many is too many?

IN MOST PEOPLE'S MINDS, THE NAME "MALTHUS" CONNECTS with the concept of overpopulation, and the adjective "Malthusian" refers to the dire consequences of reproducing to the point that we run out of resources, as predicted by the British economist Thomas Malthus in 1798. In his *Essay on the Principle of Population,* Malthus noted that populations tended to grow exponentially, so that the population increase, as measured in numbers of individuals, was greater with every new generation, whereas food supplies increased by only a constant amount over time. Eventually, Malthus reasoned, populations would outgrow their food supply, and would then become limited by disease, famine, and war.

Charles Darwin, recognizing that in nature more individuals are born than typically survive, used Malthus's idea as one of the central themes of his evolutionary theories. Ecologists have known for a long time that populations of wild plants and animals fluctuate, often dramatically, and they have studied many specific instances of this phenomenon in search of causes. The list of potential causes is fairly long, and includes everything from predators to sunspots. In addition, the ecological literature is filled with experimental studies of many kinds of plants and animals, in which the causes of population fluctuations have been either demonstrated or inferred. In these studies, some needed resource is usually shown to be a limiting factor on the population.

Ecologists also have known for a very long time that the populations of many plants and animals are relatively stable and do not necessarily undergo large fluctuations. Classic examples of such populations include the spruce and fir. But although these populations are relatively stable, they are also limited. We don't see boreal forests, for example, spreading down over the American Great Plains or the Russian steppes every year, or covering the polar ice cap one year then retreating the next. Instead, we consider them characteristic of the north, and stable enough to harvest for wood without making much of an impact on them. The first of these considerations—namely, their natural geographic distribution—is certainly correct.

In these vast conifer forests literally billions of seeds (in cones) are produced annually, but only an infinitesimal fraction of those seeds ever produce a mature, seed-bearing tree. Most of these seeds end up in places where they won't germinate—for example, in bird and rodent stomachs. So most seeds die, but some get put in the bank, so to speak—that is, the seed bank—from where they get withdrawn (germinate) under the correct conditions of moisture and temperature. Under the natural conditions that prevailed throughout most of North American history—the last fifty million years of it, at least—fires, floods, and death from disease or old age all provided an opportunity (space, time, unoccupied soil) for some of the seed-bank seeds to germinate and grow to old trees. Available moisture and temperature, produced by global climate patterns, determined the geographical extent of the spruce and fir populations; local soil and water conditions determined these populations' small-scale fluctuations as well as the survival of individual plants.

In a grand sense, therefore, prior to the arrival of humans on the North American continent, the evergreen conifer forest populations were both limited and regulated by naturally occurring events. The trees lived according to Malthusian rules. The key to understanding this fact is our ability to appreciate both the time and space scales involved in the limitations and regulations. Of course it also helps us understand population regulation if we can depersonalize the subject, which is why I started out talking about vast forests that most of us never see and that we think of (when we think about conifer forests) mainly as a source of timber. In other words, most of us don't consider the Malthusian aspects of spruce tree lives to be a moral or religious issue. The only time we ask whether there are too many spruce trees is when we are talking with a landscape architect. But obviously, throughout thousands of years of history, long before there were landscape architects, natural forces were determining that there were too many spruce trees and confining most of the survivors to the northern latitudes.

"Too many" is clearly a human idea, and it refers to the numbers that can be supported by a particular set of resources. Nature really doesn't care whether organisms live or die; only humans care. But we can explain "too many" in a rather neutral and practical way by considering what ecologists call carrying capacity. Carrying capacity is the number of organisms of a particular species that an environment can support. Two environments might have different carrying capacities for the same species; one environment might have different carrying capacities for different species. As far as nature is concerned, "too many" really means "a higher number than the carrying capacity." In the northern forest example given above, when more seeds are produced than can ever germinate and grow into an adult, then the dead seeds are those individuals produced beyond the carrying capacity of the biogeographical region we know as boreal forest. A lightning-strike fire, however, can provide a local opportunity, clearing a place for more new trees than could otherwise grow in that spot. But the burned area still has only a certain carrying capacity, and once that capacity has been achieved, the population will again be relatively stable and disturbed only by death.

This general principle of the relationship between population size and environmental carrying capacity is one of the most truly fundamental and broadly applicable ecological concepts. It applies not only to boreal forests but to individual bacteria in a test tube.

Speaking of test tubes, it's time to tell you my favorite story, namely the one about the talking bacteria. These bacteria divide once every minute and they live in a test tube that has only enough food and space in it to support this kind of reproduction for an hour. A little bit of simple math helps understand what these talking bacteria are saying. A minute after the scientist puts one bacterium into the tube, let's say at 11:00 P.M., there are two bacteria, and after another minute (two minutes into their hour), four. They can keep reproducing at this rate for an hour, so at midnight, of course, these remarkable bacteria run out of resources and die. Calculating backwards, we discover that one minute before midnight, the tube is half filled with bacteria, and two minutes before midnight, it's a fourth filled (= three-fourths empty). From 11:00 P.M. until 11:58 P.M., the bacteria have flourished, multiplied, and diversified into a large community that includes bacterial politicians, businessmen, ecologists, and of course college students (remember, it's only a story).

And what do these talking bacteria say at 11:58 P.M.? The ecologist, of course, says what ecologists have been saying for quite a while—namely, that *we're about to run out of resources.* The politician, likewise, says what politicians have been saying for quite a while, namely that *the ecologists are idiots; we have three times as many resources as we've used throughout all our history, so don't worry (and vote for me because I'm so smart).* In a similar manner, the bacterial businessman says what businessmen have been saying forever and forever, namely that *our political leaders are right; we have three times as many resources as we've used throughout all recorded history, so we should sell some to another test tube (and gimme a tax break to create the new jobs produced by these sales).* And the bacterial college student is asking what young people ask all the time, namely: *Whom should I believe?* I think we should listen to the ecologist, but I'm biased.

Obviously the tale of the talking bacteria is only a teacher's device for putting the concept of "too many" into various perspectives. I'm not entirely sure where I got this story, but it may have come from a physicist at the University of Colorado, Al Bartlett, who made a career out of analyzing our resource use. The point of the story is fairly obvious: No matter what you want to believe about the natural world, we are still very much a part of that world, and there are certain fundamental ecological principles that operate on all organisms no matter what they believe. One of these principles is that environments possess carrying capacities and will not support populations larger than those capacities, no matter what politicians and businessmen claim. The other principle is that exponential growth brings populations to their environmental carrying capacity at an increasing speed. As the talking bacteria are about to discover, in periods of exponential growth, it's fairly easy to delude oneself about just how rapidly a population is approaching its limits.

To what extent does this principle apply to humans? That is a good question with many answers. Mathematicians, as well as many college students, can easily calculate the year at which the mass of humanity comes to exceed the mass of Earth, assuming that human reproductive rates remain what they are today. It doesn't take a rocket scientist, or even a ten-minute ecologist, to figure out that some time prior to that date, humanity will begin to live a rather Malthusian existence, in which our resources become increasingly scarce. On the other hand, something may happen to stop human population growth well before it reaches the Earth's carrying capacity. Malthus thought that "something" was a combination of famine, war, and disease. Many people today believe that the "something" is technology, which won't necessarily stop our population from growing but will greatly increase, perhaps even to near infinity, Earth's carrying capacity.

Most scientists believe rather strongly that such faith in technology is perhaps not justified. Most scientists have seen too many experiments fail, had too much experience with technology that simply didn't work the way it was supposed to, to ever place complete faith in that ethereal and unpredictable phenomenon known as "technology." Most scientists, and especially most ecologists, also understand that simply being alive is not necessarily the same as being human.

Thus humans appear to need intellectual stimulation—art, music, literature, science, problems to solve, and meaningful work—in addition to bread and milk. And most ecologists understand clearly that although we may run out of bread, milk, art, and literature, we have a seemingly inexhaustible supply of problems to solve. These same ecologists also know that the problem of maintaining our humanity as we near Earth's carrying capacity is the most difficult of all the challenges in this inexhaustible supply.

15

how long is short? — or, how short is long?

FOR THIS CHAPTER, "SHORT" AND "LONG" WILL REFER TO time rather than size. In Chapter 1, "How Do We Humans View the World?" I characterized us as being shortsighted, and I hope I portrayed that characteristic as a rather natural one, of biological origin, rather than as a condemnation of attitude and behavior. I don't believe humans necessarily must act against their own best interests, however, just because they happen to have inherited a trait from their ancestors. On the other hand, humans don't always understand that "short" and "long" are relative terms, not absolute ones. For this reason, what might seem like a long time to us may be, to the planet, a virtual eye blink, and what might seem like a short time to us can be an eternity to a microorganism. Ecologists often use the term "scale" to describe their point of reference. Events that occur over the course of a minute are small-scale ones in comparison with those that occur over the course of a day. Similarly, events that occur over a ten-million-year period are large-scale ones in comparison with those that occur over our lifetimes. Ecologists, and indeed most scientists, shift their thoughts easily along these sliding relative time scales.

In fact, if I had to pick one trait that separates ecologists, and organismic biologists in general, from the rest of humanity, it would be this trait of being able to direct their thinking along several relative time scales. One of the secrets to acquiring ecological knowledge and insights is learning how to shift one's thoughts easily from today to yesterday to the middle of the next century, then back to the Pleistocene. The minds of molecular biologists—those who study, and often manipulate, large molecules such as DNA—typically don't move so easily among time scales from minutes to hundreds of millions of years. But ecologists, searching for explanations of the numerous phenomena observed in nature, must think in terms of everything from prey-predator relationships to evolutionary histories. Acts of predation, as anyone who's watched nature shows on television knows, occur over short time scales—seconds, usually; minutes or hours at most if one includes stalking or waiting for prey. Evolutionary histories, however, are played out over long periods—days to months in the case of viruses, decades in the case of some plants, and millennia for most of the rest of us. An ecologist studying the evolution of predatory behavior must of necessity compress both time scales into a single package of understanding. I don't believe ecologists are born with such abilities; like other practicing professionals, ecologists have to learn the tricks of their trade, and time-scale vision is one of those tricks.

Long and short times are also important considerations when dealing with questions of stability. Governments, cultures, religions, school athletic programs, businesses, and indeed most human organizations are concerned with stability. But stability is simply not the rule in living systems, including governments and football teams built by humans. Nor is stability the general rule, at least over the long term, in nature. And the words "long term" again raise the issue of scale. At the longest scales, we can say that no populations are stable. The vast and overwhelming majority of species that have ever lived on Earth are now extinct. But on shorter time scales, we often see that populations are relatively stable, being "regulated" by various natural processes. Such regulation involves dynamic, give-and-take interactions between organisms and their environments. Sometimes such interactions are highly complex, with multiple factors at work.

So population regulation, like all things that are dynamic and complex, is interesting especially to ecologists, whose whole business is characterized by dynamism and complexity.

Dynamism and complexity are also interesting to those whose business is business. For this reason, as well as some other, more compelling and theoretical ones, ecology and economics tend to share certain ideas, although these ideas may not be expressed in identical terms. "Supply," "growth," "capacity," and "optimal" are all terms that apply both to ecology and business. Every businessperson knows that industry relies on a supply of raw materials which in turn get converted into supplies of wholesale goods, and even those in service industries know how vital a supply of human resources is to long-term profitability. Economic growth is often expressed in terms of the changing volume of business conducted. Markets are sometimes said to be saturated, or incapable of supporting additional growth. And a businessperson who has optimized the relationships between supply and growth is doing about all he or she can to do ensure long-term survival of the company.

Similarly, populations of roadside daisies are regulated by their supply of moisture and nutrients, the growing season, the capacity of the ditch to satisfy their requirements, and the presence of other plants. And everyone knows that whatever happens to these daisies in the next few days may or may not determine what happens to them in the next few years. An ecologist tries to understand the time scales, dynamism, and complexity of events that determine whether the daisies are in the ditch tomorrow, and whether daisies will still be growing beside that road when his or her children are old enough to see them. And business executives, too, try to understand the events that determine how long the business will operate, and whether their children will have an opportunity for meaningful employment.

Ten-minute ecologists need to pay attention to issues of scale, primarily in order to understand the various resource-utilization arguments swirling around in the political arena. The economic term "growth" is probably the most important concept to apply to public discussion of ecological issues. To "grow" is to get larger; thus "growth" refers to a *process.* Anyone who's reared a child, or bought a baby puppy (or kitten) and watched it grow, knows that a 12-pound dog "grows" into a 15-pound dog, and then that same 15-pound dog grows into a 20-pound dog. The same rules apply to kids, kittens, earthworms, and elephants. In other words, growth is added on to the previous size.

Percentage growth, by which economic health is often assessed, is a very misleading indicator of anything, especially economic health. A 12-pound dog that grows 5 percent in a month adds 0.6 pound; a 15-pound dog that grows 5 percent in a month, however, adds 0.75 pound, and a healthy, growing 20-pound pup puts on a whole pound. If we're talking about the same puppy, growing at the rate of 5 percent per month, then that puppy is putting on *increasing amounts of weight (numbers of pounds) every month.* If your 20-pound puppy keeps growing at the 5 percent *rate,* then at the end of another year you'll have a 36.3-pound dog. If it has just kept putting on a pound a month, however, you'll have only a 32-pound dog. Percentage growth is the same as compound interest, and over the course of the year it gives you nearly 40 percent more puppy than you'd have if Doggy simply added its pound every month.

In most cases, on a large scale and over long time periods, percentage growth of various processes eventually brings the growing organism up against its environmental limits. Why? Because some essential resources—water, energy, food of a particular kind—are themselves typically limited, and these resources rarely if ever grow, especially not in percentage terms. If your puppy keeps growing at 5 percent per month, then after its second year it will weigh over 65 pounds and be a rather hefty playmate. But if it continues growing at that same rate for another ten years (typical life of dogs), then you've got a 6-ton dinosaur dog curled up beside the fireplace or roaming the neighborhood. Obviously something in most dogs genes stop them from growing indefinitely.

Businessmen and politicians tend to view continuous percentage growth as a sign of a healthy economy. Ecologists, however, because they tend to shift their thoughts and analyses between both short- and long-term time periods, can envision the cute baby puppy that is no sooner house-trained than it has grown into the 6-ton monster that has to be fed, housed, leashed, and made to heel and fetch a ball if it's to be kept "healthy." Percentage growth in utilization of a limited resource is one of the more easily transferred concepts. Over the short run, we usually can get by with percentage increases in consumption of limited resources, but over the long run, such utilization will inevitably bring the user up against the harsh reality of limits, whether the resource be fresh water or petroleum.

As a political aside, I've always thought it strange that people seem to have such fear of things perceived as wastes (nuclear and otherwise) and such a cavalier attitude toward resources. Thus "not in my backyard" is a rallying cry for opposition to everything from landfills to nuclear power plants, while "not in my lifetime" is an excuse for continued percentage-growth exploitation of fixed resources. Thus a radioactive isotope with a half-life of several thousand years inspires fear, even though the level of that isotope may be comparable to radioactivity in a brick house, while an essential resource with a whole life of a couple of hundred years inspires denial. Think back to the story I told in the previous chapter, in which the talking bacteria discussed their various perceptions of growth against the limited resources in their test tube. Most ecologists view Earth as simply a big test tube. And, in a sense, these scientists are correct. After all, there's no new Earth filled with fresh water, abundant petroleum, and vast continents of arable land for the taking. There's only the old Earth, which has been here for 5 billion years and has watched a long parade of life forms come and go—some, such as starfish and their relatives, lasting for several hundred million years and surviving mass extinctions, and others, such as humans, existing for only a fraction of that time and remaining untested by giant meteorites and continent-rending volcanic eruptions.

In summary, one of the tricks to becoming a ten-minute ecologist is to learn how to interpret information in terms of various time scales. This task is not a very difficult one. All you have to do is play "what if?" with all the ecological, and indeed economic, information that comes your way in newspapers, magazines, radio, and television.

1 6

what good is a
swamp?

A SWAMP IS GOOD FOR MANY REASONS, ALTHOUGH PEOPLE who are not ecologists don't often think in terms that make these reasons seem valid. Also, "swamp" can mean many things to many people. Perhaps the easiest way to define "swamp" is to equate it with "wetland." After all, a swamp is a form of wetland, although not all wetlands are what we might typically call a swamp. Some wetlands are marshes. My dictionary defines "swamp" as "a wet spongy land saturated and sometimes covered with water." "Wetland" is described as "land (such as tidal flats or swamps) containing much moisture." So I believe our equation of the two has some basis in the traditional uses of our language. The term "wetland," however, also has some fairly serious political implications, in part because of the federal government's attempts to help protect wetlands, but mostly because of the government's attempts to define exactly what they are and are not. I'm using the term "swamp" in this book because it's more fun than "wetland." "Swamp" makes me think of wading into some mucky place, having dragonflies circling around your head, finding wonderful tiny organisms, and getting real dirty. "Wetland" makes me think of politicians in three-piece suits, federal regulations, environmental extremists, and farmers with guns.

When the average citizen asks "What good is a swamp?" then that person is really asking "Of what economic value is this wetland?"

This question is a very difficult one to answer, and our satisfaction with the answers depends on our perception of economic value. For most people, economic value is short-term and immediate: a job that pays high wages, a piece of property that yields rich crops or valuable minerals, a gold ring, a Jackson Pollock painting, any specific item that can be bought or sold or provides money on a schedule that allows us to buy things like groceries, gasoline, and utility services. But ecologists tend to think in more abstract, general, and longer terms than average citizens do. Thus when you ask an ecologist "What good is a swamp?" you're likely to get an answer like "Insects are the glue that holds life on Earth together." Many people who get such answers respond with another question: "H-u-u-u-uh?"

Basically, swamps are "good" for a number of reasons, most of the important ones being philosophical, educational, and spiritual. Humans tend to have a certain intellectual relationship with their surroundings, and those who live near, or have access to, rural or wilderness areas often acquire a certain reverence for undeveloped areas such as mountains, deserts, and—yes, believe it or not—swamps. Such swamp neighbors soon learn that swamps are "good" because:

1. Swamps are places where untold numbers—literally billions and billions—of microscopic and nearly microscopic organisms live, breed, and die. These tiny organisms are near the bottom of the food pyramid (see Chapter 7, "Who Eats Whom?"), and they are eaten by equally untold numbers of larger organisms—although "larger" in this case may be somewhat of a misnomer, because down at the bottom of the food chain, even predators are sometimes quite small. So nature's terrestrial food pyramid—that is, the one operating on land—rests in part on the wetlands. Near the top of this food pyramid are birds, including migratory ones that utilize wetlands on more than one continent, eat flying, as well as nonflying, insects (mosquitoes and lawn grubs), and provide us with enormous pleasure (see #2 on the next page).

Many aquatic food pyramids also rest on wetlands adjacent to rivers, lakes, and even oceans. Wetlands bordering a lake provide shallow waters for young fish to hide in and at the same time provide a massive crop of the small insects and crustaceans that newly hatched fishes eat. After all, a 10-pound bass starts out as an almost microscopic hatchling, which in turn must find lots of even more microscopic food, while at the same time avoiding its larger hungry cousins, if it's ever to grow into that lunker being held up so proudly in the Polaroid photo by a grinning fisherman.

2. Swamps are patches of habitats where many migrating birds spend significant amounts of time. Significant may not mean weeks or months so much as feeding time. For many birds, a day in a swamp is worth a week in a less productive habitat. A good example of this dependence is the lesser sandhill crane, which migrates through the Great Plains in the spring, congregating for a month or so in a hundred-mile stretch of the Platte River in Nebraska. These cranes eat vast numbers of earthworms and snails produced in wet meadows and small "swamps" adjacent to the river. During March and early April, the skies are filled with dramatic flocks of these large birds uttering their primeval calls. The local tourist boom, produced by people from all over the world coming to places like Grand Island, Nebraska, results in a major economic benefit to the region, as well as traffic headaches for local law-enforcement officials. Scientists believe that the weight gained by these birds in March, as well as the calcium derived from snail shells, is essential to their nesting success in Canada. I cite the lesser sandhill crane because it gives us such a clear and obvious example of the major economic benefits being derived from wildlife protection, conservation, and wetlands. The main reason the example is so clear and obvious is that there is a heavy-duty advertising and crane souvenir business going on all year in that part of the country. But there are dozens, perhaps hundreds, of cases such as this one in which wetland-based ecotourism is a truly major industry.

3. Swamps are places where scientists, teachers, and students learn of the mechanisms by which nature replenishes itself and detoxifies our wastes. For this reason, to whatever extent basic knowledge about the way the planet operates is of value, to that extent swamps are also

of value. (Swamps are not alone in this regard, but they stand pretty high on the list of important types of habitat laboratories.)

Reason #3 may be the most important by far, and it applies not only to swamps, but also to many other kinds of natural areas. A ten-minute ecologist needs to remember that certain types of classrooms cannot be built. They have to be found instead. Swamps, mountain ranges, volcanoes, earthquake zones, coral reefs, prairies, and rain-forests are all good examples of such classrooms. Without them we cannot produce the scientists that give us the information necessary to make rational choices about natural-resource utilization. These scientists are our ten-year ecologists. When it comes to long-term ecological processes that affect our lives, ignorance is the most costly of luxuries, and knowledge, including that provided to researchers by readily available wetlands, is the most economical of necessities.

Generally, however, accountants, politicians, and some educational administrators are not trained to think in such terms. Accountants, politicians, and financially strapped school administrators, as well as a few other nonscientific types, also believe that real swamps can be replaced by virtual swamps, software, models, and handouts. They can't; nothing demonstrates the naïveté of this belief more than a bucket of swamp gunk and a kid who's just been asked, "What's all that stuff?" The rapidly widening young eyes, the suddenly stimulated curiosity, the excitement of pure exploration manifested in an eager mind, and the flood of questions are what every teacher lives for but so often only dreams about when instructional materials are obviously artificial, are all what a swamp is worth.

Thus one of the reasons why I wrote this book is to help this poor kid, his or her parents, and his or her teachers in their dealings with people who, for economic reasons, want to replace reality with models. This budding scientist, who eventually will contribute significantly to his or her nation's economic and political stability through research, teaching, and public service, is about to discover that the virtual-reality computer school touted so highly by various leaders, including some professional educators, is a very, and I do mean a *very,*

poor substitute for a well-educated human teacher, some good literature, an adequate microscope, some sharp dissecting tools, and a
bucket of swamp gunk.

The long-term value of natural classrooms is simply a given, although there is a constant battle between biology teachers and other
kinds of "teachers" to keep this fact in the mind of a public that seems
to outgrow its hard-earned history lessons very quickly. But those
history lessons are important indeed. First, economies and cultures
cannot be sustained over the long term unless the environments that
support them are also sustained. Second, economies and cultures are
themselves interdependent, and it is nearly impossible for cultures to
flourish when economies collapse (although flourishing economies
can produce cultures of their own). And third, water and energy are
two essential ingredients to modern, and especially industrialized,
cultures and economies; without them, the economies collapse and
drag their cultures down in the process. It's a long way, philosophi-
cally, from a wetland to the American dream, but the latter rests as
surely as a towering natural food pyramid upon knowledge of the natural world, and not only the knowledge that lets us exploit that world,
but the knowledge that warns us when we've exploited it too much.
There are few better laboratories in which to learn the latter than
your local swamp.

Reasons #1 and #2 here are actually explanations for the ecologist's
seemingly off-the-wall answer ("Insects are the glue that holds life on
Earth together") to our original question ("What good is a swamp?").
In many ways, insects *are* the glue that holds natural systems together,
and to whatever extent we humans depend on natural systems, that
bug glue holds us together, too. Insects are the primary primary consumers (sorry, couldn't pass up an opportunity to use that phrase!);
that is, the energy and materials of an ecosystem flow mainly into the
mass of insects, spiders, and other arthropods before ending up in the
larger predators such as robins and warblers.

Reason #3 explains why ten-year ecologists, and conservationists
in general, are so enamored with wetlands. Many of these people got
exposed early on to natural areas, including swamps, and learned from

firsthand experience that pictures and television are a very poor substitute for real mud that breeds both crawlies and questions. Some in the conservation movement, however, have tried to calculate the "good" of wetlands in more mundane terms, such as dollars. The results are usually startling. In a recent issue of *Audubon,* for example, Ted Williams quotes a University of California study showing that 454,000 acres of California wetlands (all that remains from well over a million acres) were worth about $10 billion a year, while the Louisiana coastal marshes contribute $2 billion a year in seafood alone (see *Audubon,* November 1996). These dollar values are usually based on a wetland's role as detoxifier of agricultural chemicals and waste, as well as basis for a local food pyramid resting beneath a commercial fishery.

In summary, swamps are good because they are so often at the base of both aquatic and terrestrial food pyramids. But swamps are also vitally important to us as living laboratories, from which our knowledge of how ecosystems work is derived.

why are ecologists
such nerds?

ECOLOGISTS ARE SUCH NERDS FOR THE SAME REASON that a large number of scientists in general are nerds—namely, because they don't give a damn about the things most of the population cares about. What *does* most of the population care about? That's a difficult question to answer without stereotyping a large number of people, and there isn't enough hard data to support any answer I might suggest. There are some pretty good data that tell us how members of the general population spend a great deal of their time and money, however, so we might conclude that most people care about those things. For example, sports is truly big business; athletics—from participation to consumption of team paraphernalia and clothing—touches all our lives from youth to old age, intrudes constantly into our living rooms through TV, and occupies much of our conversation. Similarly, newspapers, magazines, and television programs are filled with advertisements, sex, politics, crime, war, and religion.

But if you asked a large sample of ecologists, or of scientists in general, where sports, sex, politics, advertisements, and religion are on their priority lists of major concerns, my guess is that the typical answer would be "pretty far down" (if on the list at all). I might be wrong, indeed quite wrong, about sex, but not too far off on politics, advertisements, material goods (money), and religion. So if ecologists don't care much about the things most of the rest of us care deeply about, in this sense they are different from us; they make up part of what the philosophers call the other. The "other" is a general term for those who are different, whether that difference be skin color, native language, religion, sexual orientation, or opinions about natural-resource use. "Nerd" is just another word for "other."

What *do* ecologists care about? Again, we don't have a great deal of hard data, but we do have a measure of what they spend most of their time and efforts doing: teaching and research. In fact, if most of them had their way, they'd probably spend most of their time doing research in ecology and very little of their time teaching, and even far less, if any at all, on sports, politics, material wealth, and religion. From observing the behavior of numerous ecologists over several decades, I'd venture to say that if given half an opportunity most of them would depart from civilization immediately and take off for some reasonably exotic and biologically challenging part of the world to study plants and animals. When they got to this particular place, they would not play golf, seek out famous restaurants, or go windsurfing, or lie around on the beach soaking up the sun. They might spend a few evenings hanging out in a colorful local bar talking about ecology if they could find someone willing to listen. But in general they'd spend virtually all their waking hours studying plants and animals and the relationships between them. The locals would treat these ecologists with the fear, disdain, gratitude (for small amounts of money spent on food and shelter), or tolerance typically reserved for the deranged, depending on where this particular exotic place might be. The ecologists might, or might not, notice either the locals or the treatment.

Ecologists are nerds also because their minds tend to be filled with thoughts about timeless questions and natural processes that operate on a global scale. In other words, they think a lot about who eats whom, who wins competitions (in the Darwinian sense, not in the human-athletics sense), and how real estate is really divided up. What would our society be like if we had no such nerds? Pretty ignorant, to be rather brutally honest. Nerds who think a lot about timeless questions and natural processes are the source of most of our understanding about our relationships with the planet that supports us. Not all of us like that understanding, or want to hear about it, but it's part of the body of knowledge that needs to be considered when we make major decisions that alter the atmosphere or vast areas of the landscape. For if there is one thing the eco-nerds have shown us, it's that we humans do in fact have the collective power to make our planet uninhabitable.

The fact that we have such power may come as a shock to a typical citizen, but it doesn't come as a shock to any professional scientist, who by virtue of training and research knows that Earth's resources are limited. Granted, Earth is a very rich planet, with enormous resources of land, air, and water. Nevertheless, those resources are finite, and humans have demonstrated repeatedly that they can exhaust them, or use them to their limits, at least locally. It remains to be determined whether we can exhaust them globally, but few if any eco-nerds doubt that we have that ability.

Why do these people think this way? Because all of them are reasonably well trained in mathematics and perfectly able to calculate the approximate date at which we will probably run out of oil, coal, and available fresh water. While that date is fairly far off, it's only an eye blink in geological time, so these scientists, who tend to think in natural terms, consider the date rather imminent. Eco-nerds also know full well that humanity will experience truly massive misery long before our collective mass becomes equal to that of the planet. Most people don't want to hear these predictions, or think about them. And for most of us, it's easy to resolve the stress of unpleasant thoughts by calling the ecologists nerds.

The mental preoccupation with timeless questions puts ecologists in somewhat the same category as poets, other types of free thinkers, mystics, and dreamers. Indeed, many scientists could also be so characterized, although our political leaders and business executives would prefer that scientists be people who are working hard to solve practical problems and produce economic miracles. Well, some scientists do these things, occasionally on purpose. But most real scientists are like stereotypical ecologists, who in turn are not all that different from other intellectuals. Somebody has to study the various phenomena studied by nerds. Why? Because over the long haul, these folks collectively produce things that somebody on Earth needs and wants. And rarely do nerds start wars, which is probably a fairly important reason to keep them around. As an aside, wars are generally started by those who have convinced us that we simply must have whatever the war will produce.

Now that we've covered the important reasons why ecologists are nerds, I need to mention a few of the unimportant reasons, beginning with their clothing. A large percentage of male ecologists dress like outright slobs, and some of them seem to take a fair amount of pride in doing so. Do these habits make them bad people? No. But it does make the businessmen and midlevel university administrators disinclined to hang around with ecologists very much, or to treat them with a whole lot of respect in public. When it comes to scientists, businessmen and middle managers seem to prefer people with white lab coats in clean, glassware- and chemical-infested environments with radioactivity warning signs on all the doors. Should male ecologists be a little more dapper? No. If they suddenly started showing up for work dressed in three-piece suits and $50 ties, their ecologist friends would probably disown them. I certainly don't have any serious statistics on ecologists' wardrobes, of course, and such statistics probably don't exist. So these comments about clothing, and the relationship between clothing and the respect of businessmen and middle managers, are all impressions based on about thirty-five years of experience. Nevertheless, they're pretty close to target. The female ecologists seem to do a little bit better than the males in terms of clothing selection.

The other major unimportant reason why ecologists are such nerds is that most of them are employed as faculty members at colleges and universities. In American society today—for example, in movies and sitcoms—intellectuals of all kinds, and especially university professors, are portrayed as nerds.

Should we worry about these poor nerdy ecologists? Probably not; they don't do a whole lot of worrying about themselves. Should we worry about what they are telling us about planet Earth and our utilization of it? Yes. In fact, we probably should be paying a great deal of attention to what scientists in general are telling us, and a good deal less attention to what the politicians, salesmen, athletes, and ministers are telling us. But with that last bit of advice, I've crossed over the line into polemical territory. And finally, should we worry about the poor nerdy image ecologists acquire just from being intellectuals? In my opinion, yes, we should worry when our society treats as "the other" those intelligent, highly educated people who think about timeless questions.

why do scientists argue?

SCIENTISTS ARGUE FOR SEVERAL REASONS. FIRST, THEY'RE humans, and humans argue, period, about all kinds of things from politics to . . . you name it. Second, scientists argue because they tend to have strong minds and solid opinions about fairly complex matters. Put two such people in the same room, especially if they are experts on the same general phenomenon (for example, the weather), and eventually they'll find a way to express different opinions about something important to them both. Third, scientists argue about the best ways to actually conduct a scientific study. In other words, they don't always agree on the best technology to use in order to solve a problem (in this regard, scientists are similar to coaches). Fourth, scientists argue because of what they personally believe to be important questions, as opposed to unimportant questions, to address (see "strong opinions" above). Finally, and perhaps most important relative to our understanding of ecology, scientists argue because they have different interpretations of the same set of observations. Scientists may argue for many other reasons, too, but these five are certainly enough for any book entitled *10 Minute Ecologist.*

Most of the reasons listed are characteristic of the world of science, in general, not just ecology. Every scientist is quite familiar with arguments, controversies, alternative explanations for phenomena, conclusions that are shown to be false, seemingly trivial observations later shown to be quite important, and the like. Every scientist also is familiar with the underlying motivation to argue—from petty personality differences to legitimate technical alternatives for a particular study. To expand on these sources of disagreement, illustrating them with specific examples, would be to write a book on the history of science, or sociology of science, depending on which examples were chosen. The Manhattan Project, our effort to build an atomic weapon during World War II, is a great example of scientific research in which there was much at stake but in which there also were many disagreements, from personal to technical. For this reason, the Manhattan Project is an excellent case study that has been explored in numerous books and a few films.

Most projects, however, are much more mundane than the Manhattan Project. Nobody makes a feature film about some poor graduate student studying the parasites living inside an obscure beetle. And although the letters DNA are quite familiar to many of us, if for no other reason than their use in the O. J. Simpson trial and other highly publicized events (for example, the investigation to determine whether Thomas Jefferson actually sired children by a slave woman), and at times are surrounded by high drama, the truth is that the overwhelming majority of people studying DNA are doing it squirreled away in labs where they're working on pretty mundane problems with no screenplay potential. But you still hear them standing around in the halls arguing about the best way to do a particular experiment. That's because they're scientists.

Before going into some depth on scientific arguments and what they mean to a ten-minute ecologist, I need to answer a question that may be in your mind: Why would anyone work on a problem that's mundane, unglamorous, with not much at stake? This question is very easy to answer: because many such problems are great, and I do mean truly *great,* training exercises that teach a person how to do a lifetime of meaningful teaching and research as a scientist. (Many such problems are also pretty useless as training exercises, but this often gets discovered in a hurry and the problems usually get dropped.) And furthermore, many of these kinds of problems are truly captivating ones, once a person understands their biological (as opposed to human) significance. So that's why thousands of people study things politicians may not think are very important and thus perhaps don't want to support with tax money. The study of mundane problems, however, is the one activity that probably does more than anything else to ensure that our nation, with its extreme dependence on technology, has an adequate supply of trained scientists and teachers of science.

So much for science in general. Why do ecologists argue? One of the main reasons ecologists argue is that their observations are not always as unequivocal as those obtained, for example, in a canned freshman chemistry lab experiment. Phenomena such as rainfall, wind velocity, distribution of plants, activity of insects, and numbers of birds in an area are all the stock-in-trade of ecologists. But these phenomena are not always easily measured precisely, nor are experiments done outside the lab particularly easy to design and carry out. These experiments take a lot of time, patience, physical labor, and sometimes money. And to be completely honest, most wild animals are really dumb, especially insects, worms, and snails (and these, collectively, *are* most animals). Plants are not always particularly cooperative, either. Furthermore, the weather, which is about as uncontrollable as natural phenomena get, has as much effect on an ecologist's research as it does on a farmer's business. So there are a lot of ways for variation to enter an ecologist's studies, and in science, variation always, and I do mean *always,* increases the potential for serious discussion about observations.

The other reason ecologists argue is that in the past couple of decades, their observations have acquired political significance, largely because of the predictions derived from those observations. In the vast majority of scientific endeavors, observation and prediction go hand in hand as working tools. "Prediction" in this case means a testable hypothesis. Scientists, including ecologists, are very comfortable with predictions, including those that are not later supported by observation. When predictions are not later supported by data, we call this rejection of the hypothesis, and it is a highly useful and productive event in the life of most scientists. In fact, most scientists, including most ecologists, spend most of their research effort trying to reject hypotheses in order to truly test their predictions. But when the scientists, including ecologists, predict that the Earth's average temperature will rise enough to melt the ice caps, flood coastal cities (including New York, Los Angeles, and Seattle), and alter the agricultural economy of nations (such as the United States), then the testing of that hypothesis becomes a rather serious matter of interest to politicians. The testing of that prediction also becomes a scientific activity vulnerable to variation introduced by theatrics, demagoguery, lies, self-interest, and emotion.

Then, because ecologists are scientists, they suggest causes for the phenomenon of global warming (for instance, America's love affair with fossil fuels). But because of the rather dire consequences of this prediction, should it come true, ecologists, as well as atmospheric scientists, find themselves involved in politics. Accumulation of data, interpretation of data, the writing of hypotheses and predictions, and suggestions of causality are all typical daily activities of scientists, including ecologists. Politics—including theatrics, demagoguery, lies, and emotion—is not a typical daily activity of scientists. Well, at least not most scientists. Nevertheless, when scientists claim to have discovered things that large numbers of people would like to deny exist—such as ozone depletion and global warming—then scientists get dragged into arguments because of these discoveries. Depending on the significance of the discoveries, scientists also may find themselves accused of "not really proving" that something is true or highly likely. In some cases, scientists may discover that people with political agendas have gone looking for, and found, scientists who disagree with other scientists' interpretations, then used that disagreement for political purposes. Then scientific arguments get dragged out of the lab and into the public glare. At that point, the voting public needs to be very perceptive in order to distinguish the science from the politics.

But perhaps the most important reason of all that scientists argue is the fourth one given in the opening paragraph of this chapter: their differing opinions on important, versus unimportant, questions and answers. Like most areas of original intellectual endeavor—including art, music, and literature—science is guided by prevailing paradigms. Paradigms are really collections of legitimate questions and allowable answers. The questions result in part from available technology; the answers are produced by past research. The quickest way to be labeled a scientific jerk is to spend your time addressing questions that are considered illegitimate by the scientific community—for example, questions involving psychic powers or levitation. In general, scientists, including ecologists, consider questions on the legitimate list to be relatively important. In other words, these scientists are said to be "guided by the paradigms of their discipline." One of the quickest ways to start an argument among scientists, including ecologists, is to promote the importance of some question not on the legitimate list. The only way to end such an argument is to demonstrate, through research, that your previously illegitimate question is in fact an important one. When this happens, pariahs become heros and vice versa. Well, maybe it's not quite that dramatic, but to those involved in scientific arguments, these events often *seem* that dramatic.

In summary, it's important for a ten-minute ecologist to remember two things about scientific arguments: (1) they are a regular and normal aspect of science, and (2) scientists don't usually make controversial predictions without some reason (typically that reason is preliminary data or observations). Because of this, it's not always a good idea to completely ignore scientists' predictions just because these hypotheses "have not been proved." In many cases, by the time the prediction has been adequately tested ("proved"), the damage the scientist was predicting has already been done.

1 9

do we humans live by the same rules as beetles?

YES, HUMANS AND BEETLES BOTH HAVE LITTLE CHOICE but to live by the same rules that govern all life on Earth: We're born (or hatched, in the case of beetles), live for a relatively short period, reproduce if we can, then die. The difference between humans and beetles lies in the activities we engage in during the relatively short period that we live. But then the differences between two species of beetles, aside from their structural differences, also lie in the activities they engage in during their relatively short lives. The same things could be said of any two individual beetles, except that their individual lives (as opposed to the lives of their kind) are partly governed by chance events, over which they have no control. And the same can be said for any two individual humans, including the bit about chance events over which they have no control. So yes, humans and beetles—in fact *all* of us that occupy planet Earth—live by these same rules.

Humans, like beetles, must find food, water, and shelter in order to live from day to day. This simple rule is obvious to all of us. What's not obvious to all of us, or at least doesn't seem to be so obvious, is that we must obey this rule just the way beetles must obey it. The vast majority of human time is spent searching for food, water, and shelter, although we often call this search work or a job. Many of our most pressing human problems are linked to the search for food, water, and shelter. Unemployment, poverty, public education, agricultural politics, the illegal drug trade, illegal immigration, clearing of tropical forests, clear-cutting of timber, and a long list of other phenomena that we read about in the newspaper are all associated with the search for food, water, and shelter. That last statement might seem like a violation of my claim of neutrality in the eco-polemics wars, but it's not a violation of that claim so much as it is a rather philosophical, and somewhat detached, view of our general situation here on Earth. We take resources from the planet, spending time and effort to do so, and convert those resources into human tissue. And some of us do it more successfully than others. The same could be said for beetles.

Unlike beetles, however, humans spend a fair amount of time searching for "meaning" as well as for food, water, and shelter. For humans as a whole, "meaning" has many definitions, so not surprisingly, the search has just as many outcomes. To most people, this particular search leads them toward religion; for others, it leads to encounters with drugs, alcohol, athletics, art, music, literature, money, or political power, to mention a few ends. Thus because of our evolved traits, our massive and complex central nervous system, and our subsequently evolved culture, our lives are governed, in part, by rules that beetles, insofar as we know, don't have to follow. Beetles don't spend their lives in search of "meaning." Beetles don't have to live by the rules of speed limits. They don't have to wear clothes in public. But we still have to live by the basic beetle rules involving food, water, and shelter. As a *species* we have to live by the ultimate living organism rule, too: reproduce or die out. So aside from this business of "meaning," we're pretty much in the same category as beetles. We too are animals moving around over the face of Earth looking for food, water, and shelter.

There are about a quarter of a million known species of beetles, so by inference they find food in about that many different kinds of ways. There are also uncountable billions of beetle individuals out there looking for food, and not infrequently they find it in human cupboards, grain bins, and warehouses. Across the face of the Earth, there are 5.8 billion humans out there looking for food, and these billions of people also obtain food in a remarkable number of ways. If humans have enough money, they typically find their food in a local store or market. That statement sounds almost trivial and dumb, but what passes for food in a local store or market, and what that "food" goes through prior to arriving at the market, are both highly dependent on climate, geography, and culture. As I've indicated in other chapters, global events such as past continental drift and prevailing winds tend to dictate agricultural economies. At least to some extent, those same events probably contribute quite a bit to local culture. For example, gauchos and cowboys are independently evolved economic and cultural lifestyles associated with particular agricultural practices in similar habitats.

Modern transportation and shipping have erased many of the effects local agriculture has on the search for food. One can buy a fast-food franchise hamburger in most parts of the world, for example, or fresh ocean fish deep in the heart of a large continent. Prior to the invention of the airplane, the Sioux Indians sure never picked up a live Maine lobster, but now you can do it any day of the week in Omaha. Conversely, if Formosan aborigines, inhabitants of the island we now call Taiwan, made noodles five hundred years ago, they made them out of something other than the Kansas wheat they may use today. And if one delves further back into human history, especially into the Middle Ages and into contemporary aboriginal cultures, the relationship between local geography and feeding habits becomes reasonably obvious. Yes, without modern transportation, we seek food in our immediate surroundings, just like beetles. Ten-year ecologists who study global energy supplies foresee a time that we may well return to such beetle-like, highly localized agricultural economies.

Humans do differ from beetles in one other important way, however: People generally don't get eaten by birds and other relatively large animals, although once in a while, of course, you read about people being attacked by a mountain lion or bear, usually while they are engaged in some recreational pursuit like camping or horseback riding. But humans do get infected with viruses, bacteria, fungi, and various kinds of animal parasites like nematodes and tapeworms, just as beetles do. Humans play host to at least 250 different kinds of animal parasites alone (worms, lice, ticks, fleas, etc.). When the viruses, bacteria, and fungi (e.g., athlete's foot) are added, the list gets considerably longer. So quite literally we do get eaten by other organisms who by definition live at a higher trophic level than we do (see Chapter 7, "Who Eats Whom?"), and so most certainly we are prey as well as predator.

The "reproduce or die out" rule that applies to all *species* is one of the most interesting of all rules in biology. Why is it so interesting? Because it's the ultimate species-level paradox: Everyone has to follow it, but there are at least as many ways to follow it as there are species! I say "at least" because with the smarter species (humans, chimpanzees, elephants, whales, and the like) there are many individual variations on the species' theme. Come to think of it, there are individual variations on species' themes in lots of dumber animals, too—for example, when fruit flies of a certain genetic makeup can't sing the right mating song. What happens to fruit flies with the "wrong" genetic makeup? They miss out on a lot of fly sex, that's what happens. And tragically (yes, tragically—I am being serious for a moment), the most effective way for a human to miss out on a lot of sex is to be born with a genetic makeup that makes him or her unattractive to other human beings. On the positive side, however (I'm still being serious), human attractiveness is very often quite negotiable, an option that neither fruit flies nor beetles enjoy.

Right now, humans and many species of beetles (insofar as we know) are both reproducing quite nicely, thank you, and are in no danger of dying out as a species. But we are also clearing the tropical forests at the rate of about a hundred acres a minute, and that's where most beetles, and indeed most plants and animals of all kinds, live. So in order to satisfy our beetle-like rules (find food, shelter, water, and a mate or mates), we're eliminating the places where literally thousands of species of beetles are doing, or at least trying to do, the same thing. Indeed, instead of thousands, the numbers of beetle species being deprived of food, water, shelter, and mate(s) may easily number in the hundreds of thousands. How do we arrive at this conclusion? Easy. From the rate at which new species are being discovered, the number of scientists now describing species, and the particular beetles being studied, we can estimate the number of species yet to be discovered. It remains to be seen whether we ultimately will have to live by beetle rules in the tropics, whether we, like the beetles, will wander the charred ground, when the forests are gone, looking unsuccessfully for food, water, and shelter. We'll probably find mates. We always seem to find someone to mate with, no matter how miserable our circumstances.

So, in summary, yes indeed, we do live by the same rules as beetles, as well as some rules of our own, but technology has given us the power to forestall the application of a few of those rules. We don't know whether we can avoid living like beetles forever, and indeed, "environmental controversies" are often a product of differing opinions on just how long "forever" is.

2 0

did god make the earth in seven days?

IF A GOD MADE THE EARTH, HE/SHE/IT CONSTRUCTED THE planet over a 4- to 5-billion-year period, using the full suite of natural processes that humans have discovered over the past two or more millennia. These processes include all the astronomical, geological, atmospheric, and biological ones mentioned in any halfway decent freshman science text, plus perhaps some yet to be discovered ones. So, no, God did not make the Earth in seven days. You can believe anything you want about the origin of Earth, or the origin of all the surface features on it, including ourselves, but the vast preponderance of scientific evidence indicates that the Earth is about 4.6 billion years old and that all of us evolved on it. (There is, by the way, no evidence whatsoever for the existence of any other planets *just like Earth* in the universe. Although there is plenty of evidence that planets exist, and some well-founded speculation about the potential number of inhabited planets in the universe, insofar as we know for certain we're alone and unique—enough of a reason for wonder and spirituality, but not enough of a reason to dismiss out of hand the past two millennia of scientific observation about Earth and its origins and to attribute our existence to some recent intervention by the supernatural.)

Why does a ten-minute ecologist need to know something about the origin of Earth and its inhabitants? Because geophysical and biological processes have been at work here for several billion years, and they are still at work to produce the environment in which we, and all the other inhabitants of the planet, live. These processes range from the local to the cosmic, from the drifting of continents to the falling of meteorites, from volcanoes, floods, and earthquakes to sunspot cycles, from algal blooms to the burning of fossil fuels. Knowledge of these processes in no way diminishes the wonder anyone must have for the complexity and beauty of Earth. Such knowledge, however, does tend to emphasize both our uniqueness, and more significantly, our common interest in the health of our planet. That common interest demands that our collective political, economic, and agricultural actions maximize the Earth's ability to recover from the use we make of it. This interest also demands that we minimize our own impact on Earth's resources of land, plants, animals, minerals, water, and air, which is, of course, the same thing as maximizing the planet's ability to recover from our actions. As any ecologist, myself included, will tell you, political and economic stability, standard of living, and cultural richness all depend on long-term sustainable use of our environment. The preceding sentence is not a polemical statement as much as it is an observed fact.

How *was* Earth made? Available evidence indicates it condensed from a cloud of gas and other particles not long after the sun itself was formed from a larger cloud of gas, or perhaps as a consequence of the sun's formation. Although, of course, no one has ever watched the complete formation of a star and its planets from beginning to end, modern astronomers have studied star formation and evolution extensively using a variety of means, including space telescopes such as the Hubble. (No one has ever literally watched a chemical reaction take place, either, although, as in the case of planets and galaxies, lots of us have watched the results of chemical reactions.) Astronomers also have behaved as most scientists do by developing theories, designing instruments to help test these theories, and making the measurements necessary to test their predictions and hypotheses. As a result of all this activity, we know a great deal about the sun, the solar system, the Milky Way galaxy, and the rest of the universe. Their conclusion, so far, is that Earth began in a gas cloud about 4.6 billion years ago.

Geophysicists, likewise, have behaved about like other scientists in developing theories, making predictions based on these theories, then designing studies and instruments to test the predictions. Geophysicists tell us that the Earth's crust is made from a number of plates that "float" on the molten rock below. These plates not only carry the continents, but they also move around, drift apart or together, and bump into one another, their edges slipping beneath or riding up over other edges—in all the processes that ultimately produce earthquakes and volcanoes. The moving of plates also produces vast changes in the climate, flora, and fauna of a region, but over long periods of time. When a continent drifts, plants, animals, and microbes go along for the ride, sometimes to parts of Earth that, because of latitude and a tilted axis of rotation, may not be overly hospitable. Thus when a continent drifts from the tropics to the poles, organisms on that continent must adapt, in the evolutionary sense, or become extinct.

Some species, such as barn owls and barn swallows, are quite capable, even today, of traveling quickly between continents, so that the drifting doesn't split and isolate barn swallow and barn owl populations in quite the same way that the same process tends to break up such populations as freshwater fishes. But for most of Earth's history and most of Earth's organisms, continental drift has been a major factor in producing our present-day diversity and distribution of plants and animals. Cichlid fishes, for example, which are members of a freshwater family, evolved on a continent that later split into Africa and South America. As a result of the split and subsequent drift, cichlid fishes are found naturally in those two now widely separated places. This kind of distribution is typical of the observations used to support theories of continental drift early in this century. In the case of Africa and South America, of course, the coastline profiles also suggested a breakup far in the prehistoric past. Modern geophysics has since confirmed what the turn-of-the-century biogeographers suspected—that the two continents were once joined.

One of the most significant of the ancient geological events is known as the breakup of Pangea. Pangea is the name of a single continent that was formed about 400 million years ago from the collision of all the rest of the world's ancient continents, including Gondwana and Laurentia. Dinosaurs flourished on Pangea. About 135 million years ago, Pangea started to break apart, and over the next hundred million years broke into several other continents that ultimately drifted to their present positions. We now call these continents Africa, Eurasia, North America, South America, Antarctica, and Australia. Thus the present distribution of plants and animals is partly a result of having had ancestors who lived on Pangea; these ancestors subsequently rode a part of Pangea to its present position while evolving along the way.

Today we can see the results of all these seemingly (to us) slow geological and biological processes at work. For example, the marsupials (pouched mammals such as kangaroos) became geographically isolated from the rest of the world and remained so; this isolation was a major factor in their evolutionary history. When we go to the zoo and marvel at the wondrous Australian fauna, we're actually reacting intellectually to the geological and evolutionary events of the past 50 million years. Those events not only produced kangaroos, wallabies, koalas, and all their relatives, but also kept them isolated from the pre-dogs and pre-cats, which evolved into jackals, lions, and tigers. In the past three hundred years, the British colonized Australia, starting with the transportation of criminals, cats, dogs, and rats to the continent. That colonization was the beginning of our biological knowledge of the isolated continent. Had the Australian aborigines sent their criminals to North America by the shipload, then followed as administrators, tourists, and businessmen, there might well be outback zoos filled with marvelous exotic animals such as wolves, bison, wild turkeys, and deer. But that didn't happen. Instead, the British colonized Australia and *we* are the ones who are fascinated by that continent's exotic fauna. And a ten-minute ecologist now knows that we're fascinated by kangaroos at the zoo because they are a product of geophysical and evolutionary events that occurred over the past millions of years, far away from our familiar flora and fauna.

The evolution of the Australian fauna and flora, the extinction of the dinosaurs, the distribution of cichlid fishes, the distribution of landmasses and oceans—all are examples of "the way the universe works." Science seeks explanations for "the way the universe works," or natural phenomena. We know that the phrase "natural phenomena" includes everything from the formation of galaxies to the innermost functions of a cell. And we also know that scientists study the universe at all these levels, from the grand and cosmic to the detailed and microscopic. The ecologists have focused their attention on the mechanisms that produce and maintain the diversity of life on Earth, with special emphasis on the interactions between organisms—including humans—and their environments. There is a compelling reason for such study, and that is the shared obligate relationship we hold with the only planet in the universe actually known to support life.

My hope is that this small volume will serve to inform its readers of the many facets of that relationship and that such information will be of eventual use to us all. As we have learned so often in the past, ignorance is far more dangerous than understanding. But *10 Minute Ecologist* is only an introduction to the vast body of knowledge about our planet. Wading through the suggested readings (page 123) will be a little like wading through a swamp, in that you'll find everything in that list from organisms to philosophy. If *10 Minute Ecologist* has done its job, then that list of readings will share one other attribute of swamps: the fascination they hold for those who've ventured into them out of curiosity. And like an unrepentant naturalist, you'll go looking for more.

ABIOTIC FACTORS. Nonliving components of Earth—for example, wind, soil, water, light, and various chemical elements.

ALGAE. Several groups of photosynthetic organisms, many consisting of only a single cell, most living in water, and all lacking the tissues that transport fluids in nonalgae plants, such as those in the familiar neighborhood trees.

ARITHMETIC GROWTH. Growth in which change in numbers or size is a constant, regardless of the previous number or size, as in a payroll deduction applied to a savings account.

ATMOSPHERE. The layers of gases that surround Earth.

BACTERIA. Single-celled, microscopic organisms without a true cell nucleus surrounded by a membrane, and lacking the well-formed intracellular structures typical of plant and animal cells.

BALEEN WHALES. Whales that strain their food from the ocean, using sheets of tissue that hang down from the roof of their mouth as a strainer.

BEETLES. Exceedingly numerous insects of the order Coleoptera, which typically possess front wings hardened into covers.

BIODIVERSITY. The variety of living organisms; the number of species.

BIOME. A type of environment distinguished by its characteristic temperature, available moisture, and dominant vegetation.

BIOTIC FACTORS. The living organisms of Earth, as well as the nonliving products of living organisms, including shells, feces, skeletons of dead animals, and fallen leaves.

BLUBBER. A layer of fatty tissue beneath the skin of marine mammals such as whales and walruses.

glossary

BOREAL. Northern, particularly the forested regions of the high latitudes of the northern hemisphere.

BRACKISH (WATER). Water that is partly salty, usually resulting from the mixing of seawater and freshwater, as at the mouth of a river that empties into the ocean.

CARNIVORE. Meat-eating animal; a secondary consumer.

CLASS. One of the taxonomic groups in a biological classification (contains one or more orders, and is a member of a phylum).

CLIMAX VEGETATION. The stable, dominant type of vegetation that occupies a particular area and is determined largely by temperature and available moisture.

COMMUNITY. All the species that occupy a particular habitat and presumably interact in some way; an ecologist may selectively refer to some of those species—for example, "the plant community" or "the parasite community."

COMPETITION. An ecological interaction in which organisms attempt to obtain, or occupy, a limited, shared resource such as space, water, or food.

CONIFER. Evergreen, cone-bearing trees such as spruce, fir, and pines.

CONSUMER. An organism that eats another, typically another species, thereby obtaining energy and nutrients.

CONTINENTAL DRIFT. A geological process in which continents move across the face of the Earth because the crustal plates upon which these continents rest are themselves moving.

CRUSTACEANS. Arthropods such as crabs, crayfish, shrimp, lobsters, and tens of thousands of related forms, with two pairs of antennae and appendages with two branches.

DECOMPOSERS. Organisms, such as fungi and certain bacteria, that break down biological materials. Decomposers digest dead plants and animals.

DESCRIBER. The individual who is given credit for formally describing a species in a publication.

DIATOM. One of the types of algae; diatoms build intricate shells made of silicon.

DIVERSITY INDEX. A mathematical expression that summarizes the relative diversity of a community.

DIVISION. A large, relatively inclusive, taxonomic group used by botanists; equivalent to a phylum (used by zoologists).

DNA. The large, coiled molecule that contains genetic information.

EARTHWORMS. Segmented animals of the phylum Annelida, class Oligochaeta, that dwell in the soil.

ECOLOGICAL NICHE. A "place" in nature occupied by a particular species. This "place" consists of all the resources the species needs in order to survive.

ECOLOGIST. A scientist who studies the interactions between organisms and their environments.

ECOLOGY. The study of the interaction between organisms and their environments, with the intent of discovering how the number and distribution of organisms are maintained and controlled.

ECOSYSTEM. All the organisms, their interactions, and the environment that supports them, usually within a large, distinctly recognizable area—such as prairie, desert, or rainforest.

ENDANGERED SPECIES. A species with a population so small that the species is in danger of becoming extinct.

ENZYMES. Proteins that aid in carrying out chemical processes such as digestion.

EPIPHYTE. A plant that typically grows on another plant and obtains its moisture from the air.

EVOLUTION. Genetic changes leading to the formation of new species that occur in populations of organisms over extended periods of time.

EXPONENTIAL GROWTH. Growth in which change in numbers or size is a percentage of the previous number or size, as in compound interest applied to a savings account.

EXTINCT. No longer present as a species on Earth.

FOOD CHAIN. A linked series of feeding relationships, in which organisms feed on other organisms but are in turn fed on by still other organisms.

FOOD WEB. A group of linked and intercrossing food chains, with opportunistic feeding perhaps at several trophic levels.

FOSSIL FUEL. Coal, oil, and natural gas, all derived from plants that grew millions of years ago.

FUNGI. The mushrooms, toadstools, and similar smaller organisms that require living or once-living materials as food, function mainly as decomposers, and reproduce both sexually and asexually.

GENUS (PL. GENERA). A category in the biological classification scheme— more inclusive than the species, less inclusive than the family. A genus contains one or more species.

GEOPHAGY. The practice of eating dirt (on purpose). Also called chthonophagia.

GLACIATION. The advance of glaciers to cover parts of the Earth.

glossary

GREENHOUSE GASES. Several gases that accumulate in the upper atmosphere and prevent heat loss from Earth.

GUILD. A group of species competing for the same resource.

HABITAT. The general type of environment occupied by a species—for example, stream, lake, forest, grassland, ocean, tide pool.

HERBIVORE. An animal that eats plants; a primary consumer.

HETEROGENEITY. Literally, "the quality of being different." In the biological sense, heterogeneity refers to the extent to which a group or a habitat is characterized by differences.

HIERARCHY. In biology, a classification system with groups that are increasingly inclusive, with less inclusive groups existing only as components of the more inclusive groups.

HIGHER TAXA. The more inclusive taxonomic groups, such as phyla, divisions, classes, and orders.

HOMOGENEITY. Literally, "the quality of being the same." In the biological sense, homogeneity refers to the extent to which a group or a habitat is characterized by sameness.

INTERBREED. To reproduce sexually with one another. Members of the same species interbreed by definition; members of different species sometimes successfully interbreed.

INTERSPECIFIC. Between different species.

INTRASPECIFIC. Among members of the same species.

KRILL. Small shrimplike crustaceans that feed mainly on phytoplankton and occur in very large numbers in the ocean.

LICHENS. Organisms consisting of a species of fungus and a species of algae living in a symbiotic relationship.

LOAM. A relatively loose soil type with organic material, sand, and clay.

LOESS. Yellowish, loamlike soil generally considered to be originally deposited by the wind.

LOWER TAXA. The less inclusive taxonomic groups, such as genera and species.

MICROBE. A microscopic organism—usually bacteria, some fungi, and viruses.

MICROORGANISM. A broader, more inclusive category than that of microbes—usually microscopic plants and animals as well as bacteria and fungi.

MORAINE. A ridge of rock left behind when a glacier melts.

MUTATION. A change—especially a heritable, spontaneous change—in the genetic makeup of an organism.

NERD. A person the general public thinks of as strange, often preoccupied with arcane subjects such as math, science, ecology, and computers.

NICHE. *See* ecological niche.

NITROGEN. One of the chemical elements; the major atmospheric gas on Earth.

ORDER. One of the taxonomic groups in a biological classification (contains one or more families and is a member of a more inclusive class).

ORGANIC. Derived from living organisms such as plants, animals, bacteria, and fungi.

ORGANISM. A living entity or being.

OXYGEN. One of the chemical elements; the second most common atmospheric gas on Earth; a gas required for life as we know it.

OZONE. A gas made of three oxygen atoms. Ozone in the upper atmosphere blocks ultraviolet radiation from falling on Earth.

PARADIGM. A concept or theory that guides our thinking, mainly by establishing a range of legitimate questions and legitimate answers.

PARASITE. An organism that can exist only by living in a close, dependent, sometimes harmful relationship with another, unrelated organism.

PARENT ROCK. The rock that wears down to produce a particular soil.

PARTICLE-SIZE DISTRIBUTION. The relative numbers of soil particles, of various sizes, in a sample.

PHARMACEUTICAL. A chemical substance with medicinal properties, a drug.

PHEROMONES. "Odorless" molecules that are released by animals and in turn stimulate other members of the species to behave in certain ways.

PHLOEM. One of the plant tissues, made of tubelike cells, that function to transport fluids and sugars.

PHOTOSYNTHESIS. The biochemical process by which green plants capture the sun's energy and use that energy to build complex molecules such as sugars.

PHYLUM. A taxonomic group of animals, very inclusive, and containing all the animals that possess a similar general body plan.

PHYTOPLANKTON. Relatively small, photosynthsizing organisms—for example, floating algae—that occupy the open water in lakes and in the ocean.

PIONEER. An organism that is among the first to occupy a disturbed area. Pioneers have such properties as small, windblown seeds that aid them in finding such disturbances.

glossary

PLANKTON. Relatively small plants and animals that live suspended in water, either in the ocean or in bodies of freshwater.

PLEISTOCENE. A period of Earth's history, from about 1.7 million years to 10,000 years ago, characterized by advancing and retreating glaciers.

POPULATION. The number of freely and commonly interbreeding individuals of a species. Species can occur in more than one population, and in this case, interbreeding between the two populations may not be particularly free and common.

POSITIVE FEEDBACK SYSTEM. Any process in which the product of that process makes the process itself operate faster. A negative feedback system operates in the opposite manner (products inhibit the process).

PRODUCERS. Green plants that trap the sun's energy and use that energy to build complex molecules that in turn can be used by other organisms.

REEF. A rocklike deposit occurring in warm, shallow seas and consisting mainly of the skeleton produced by marine animals of the phylum Cnidaria (corals and their relatives).

REPRODUCTIVE ISOLATION. A condition in which groups of organisms, the same or different species, are unable to successfully interbreed with one another for any of a variety of reasons.

ROTIFERS. Microscopic animals occurring in water and moist soils, and characterized by an external cuticle made of telescoping rings, a two-lobed rear end, and bands of cilia at the front end.

SEED BANK. The seeds that are buried in soil and able to germinate if moved to the proper depth and provided with adequate moisture.

SPECIES (PL. SPECIES). The fundamental unit of biological classification. A species is a kind of organism, typically distinguished structurally, usually incapable of interbreeding with other species, and considered to have evolved from a single ancestral species.

SUCCESSION. A phenomenon in which, over time, a series of species, each with differing characteristics, dominates a disturbed area and is subsequently replaced by other species.

SYMBIONTS. Organisms that live in and on other organisms—for example, parasites.

SYSTEMATICS. The science of classification as it is applied to questions of evolutionary relationships.

TARDIGRADES. Microscopic animals, also called water bears because of their superficial resemblance to teddy bears. Tardigrades often live in moist soil.

TAXONOMY. The science of classification. Taxonomists classify organisms and study the basis for such classification.

TIDE POOL. A pool of ocean water left along the shore when the tide goes out.

TRADE WINDS. Relatively constant winds that blow mainly over the ocean from the northeast or southeast and toward the equator.

TRANSPIRATION. A process by which plants lose water, by means of evaporation, through stems and leaves.

TROPHIC. Of or relating to feeding.

TROPHIC LEVEL. A measure of the number of times energy is transformed before it is stored in an organism. This number of transformations is determined by the number of steps in a food chain.

TROPHIC PYRAMID. A picture of the energy loss that occurs when energy is transformed between trophic levels. This picture shows that most of the energy stored at one trophic level—for example, as producer green plants—is lost when the plants are converted into primary consumer herbivores. Thus the top layers of this pyramid are smaller than the bottom layers.

TROPHIC RELATIONSHIP. A relationship between organisms, usually between different species, characterized by feeding. In a trophic relationship, one species eats another.

TROPICS. The Earth's warm regions between the Tropic of Cancer and the Tropic of Capricorn.

UNDESCRIBED SPECIES. A species that has not been formally recognized by the scientific community because it has not been described, according to the rules of nomenclature, in a publication.

VAGILITY. The inherent ability of an organism to disperse geographically.

VIRUS. A parasitic microbe typically consisting of genetic information covered with a protein coat; viruses exist and reproduce only by infecting other organisms.

XYLEM. One of the plant tissues that transport water and dissolved minerals and provide structural support to plant stems.

ZOOPLANKTON. Relatively small animals that occupy open water in lakes and in the ocean.

SUGGESTED READINGS

THE FOLLOWING LIST IS INTENDED TO BE ONLY AN introduction to environmental literature that might be available in bookstores and libraries. Most of these works are relatively easy to understand and provide information that will put the information in *10 Minute Ecologist* into a broader context. Anyone who undertakes a serious program of ecological self-education will immediately discover a rich and voluminous literature on nature, including works that may be exceedingly useful but are not on this list. Eventually, however, such an explorer will encounter some of the more technical material, including modern texts. My advice is to not be intimidated. It's important that we all try to become better educated in the ecological sense, and the acts of reading, exploring the available literature and Internet resources, and talking about ecological issues are all vital to both our long-term well-being and the solution of immediate political and economic problems involving natural resources.

Abbey, E. 1968. *Desert Solitaire: A Season in the Wilderness.* New York: Ballantine Books. 303 pp.
Akin, W. E. 1990. *Global Patterns: Climate, Vegetation, and Soils.* Norman, OK: University of Oklahoma Press. 370 pp.
Bass, R. 1995. *The Lost Grizzlies: A Search for Survivors in the Wilderness of Colorado.* Boston: Houghton Mifflin Company. 190 pp.

suggested readings

Bergman, C. 1996. *Orion's Legacy: A Cultural History of Man as Hunter*. New York: Dutton. 368 pp.

Berry, W. 1981. *Recollected Essays 1965–1980*. San Francisco: North Point Press. 340 pp.

———. 1986. *The Unsettling of America: Culture and Agriculture*. San Francisco: Sierra Club Books. 228 pp.

Bowden, C. 1986. *Blue Desert*. Tucson, AZ: University of Arizona Press. 179 pp.

Brown, L. R. 1995. *Who Will Feed China? Wake-up Call for a Small Planet*. New York: W. W. Norton. 163 pp.

Buchmann, S. L., and G. Nabhan. 1996. *The Forgotten Pollinators*. Washington, DC: Island Press. 292 pp.

Campbell, D. G. 1992. *The Crystal Desert: Summers in Antarctica*. Boston: Houghton Mifflin Company. 308 pp.

Carson, R. 1951. *The Sea Around Us*. New York: Oxford University Press. 230 pp.

———. 1962. *Silent Spring*. Boston: Houghton Mifflin Company. 368 pp.

Davidson, J. W., and J. Rugge. 1988. *Great Heart: The History of a Labrador Adventure*. New York: Viking. 385 pp.

Dillard, A. 1974. *Pilgrim at Tinker Creek*. New York: Harper's Magazine Press. 271 pp.

———. 1981. *Teaching a Stone to Talk: Expeditions and Encounters*. New York: Harper and Row. 177 pp.

Dörner, Dietrich. 1996 (American edition). *The Logic of Failure: Why Things Go Wrong and What We Can Do to Make Them Right*. New York: Metropolitan Books, Henry Holt and Company. 222 pp.

Dowie, M. 1995. *Losing Ground: American Environmentalism at the Close of the Twentieth Century*. Cambridge, MA: The MIT Press, Cambridge. 317 pp.

Eiseley, L. 1946. *The Immense Journey*. New York: Random House. 210 pp.

———. 1964. *The Unexpected Universe*. New York: Harcourt Brace Jovanovich. 239 pp.

Elder, J. 1994. *Family of Earth and Sky: Indigenous Tales of Nature from Around the World*. Boston: Beacon. 323 pp.

Farb, P. 1968. *Man's Rise to Civilization as Shown by the Indians of North America from Primeval Times to the Coming of the Industrial State*. New York: Dutton. 332 pp.

———. 1978. *Humankind*. Boston: Houghton Mifflin Company. 528 pp.

Finch, R., and J. Elder. 1990. *The Norton Book of Nature Writing*. New York: W. W. Norton. 921 pp.

Gould, S. J. 1989. *Wonderful Life: The Burgess Shale and the Nature of History*. New York: W. W. Norton. 347 pp.

Gruchow, P. 1988. *The Necessity of Empty Places.* New York: St. Martin's Press. 291 pp.

Hay, J., and P. Farb. 1966. *The Atlantic Shore: Human and Natural History from Long Island to Labrador.* New York: Harper and Row. 246 pp.

Hoagland, E. 1988. *The Best of Edward Hoagland: Essays from Twenty Years.* New York: Summit Books. 429 pp.

Ives, J. D., B. R. Graham, and D. K. Alford. 1974. *Arctic and Alpine Environments.* New York: Harper & Row. 999 pp.

Janovy, J., Jr. 1978. *Keith County Journal.* New York: St. Martin's Press. 210 pp.

———. 1980. *Yellowlegs.* New York: St. Martin's Press. 192 pp.

———. 1981. *Back in Keith County.* New York: St. Martin's Press. 179 pp.

———. 1985. *On Becoming a Biologist.* New York: Harper & Row. 160 pp.

———. 1992. *Vermilion Sea: A Naturalist's Journey in Baja California.* Boston: Houghton Mifflin. 226 pp.

———. 1994. *Dunwoody Pond: Reflections on the High Plains Wetlands and the Cultivation of Naturalists.* New York: St. Martin's Press. 288 pp.

Kittredge, W. 1987. *Owning It All.* St. Paul, MN: Graywolf Press. 182 pp.

Krebs, C. J. 1988. *The Message of Ecology.* New York: HarperCollins. 195 pp.

Krutch, J. W. 1969. *The Best Nature Writing of Joseph Wood Krutch.* New York: William Morrow. 384 pp.

Leopold, A. 1949. *A Sand County Almanac, with Other Essays on Conservation from Round River.* New York: Oxford University Press. 269 pp.

Logan, W. B. 1995. *Dirt: The Ecstatic Skin of the Earth.* New York: Riverhead Books. 202 pp.

Lopez, B. 1986. *Arctic Dreams: Imagination and Desire in a Northern Landscape.* New York: Charles Scribner's Sons. 464 pp.

Lyon, T. J. 1989. *This Incomparable Land: A Book of American Nature Writing.* Boston: Houghton Mifflin. 495 pp.

Madsen, J. 1982. *Where the Sky Began: Land of the Tallgrass Prairie.* Boston: Houghton Mifflin. 321 pp.

Maser, C. 1989. *Forest Primeval: The Natural History of an Ancient Forest.* San Francisco: Sierra Club Books. 282 pp.

Matthiessen, P. 1991. *African Silences.* New York: Random House. 225 pp.

McPhee, J. 1980. *Basin and Range.* New York: Farrar, Straus, and Giroux. 216 pp.

———. 1982. *In Suspect Terrain.* New York: Farrar, Straus, and Giroux. 210 pp.

———. 1986. *Rising from the Plains.* New York: Farrar, Straus, and Giroux. 214 pp.

———. 1989. *The Control of Nature.* New York: Farrar, Straus, and Giroux. 272 pp.

suggested readings

———. 1993. *Assembling California.* New York: Farrar, Straus, and Giroux. 304 pp.

Mayr, E. 1982. *The Growth of Biological Thought.* Cambridge, MA: Belknap Press (Harvard University Press). 974 pp.

———. 1988. *Toward a New Philosophy of Biology: Observations of an Evolutionist.* Cambridge, MA: Belknap Press (Harvard University Press). 564 pp.

Nabhan, G. 1985. *Gathering the Desert.* Tucson, AZ: University of Arizona Press. 209 pp.

———. 1993. *Counting Sheep: Twenty Ways of Seeing Desert Bighorn.* Tucson, AZ: University of Arizona Press. 261 pp.

Nishizawa, T., and J. I. Uitto, eds. 1995. *The Fragile Tropics of Latin America: Sustainable Management of Changing Environments.* New York: United Nations University Press. 325 pp.

Owen, D. F. 1976. *Animal Ecology in Tropical Africa.* San Francisco, CA: W. H. Freeman. 122 pp.

Perry, R. 1973. *The Polar Worlds.* New York: Taplinger. 316 pp.

Quammen, D. 1996. *The Song of the Dodo: Island Biogeography in an Age of Extinctions.* New York: Scribners. 702 pp.

Reisner, M. 1986. *Cadillac Desert: The American West and Its Disappearing Water.* New York: Viking. 582 pp.

Reisner, M., and S. Bates. 1990. *Overtapped Oasis: Reform or Revolution for Western Water.* Washington, DC: Island Press. 200 pp.

Remmert, H. 1980. *Arctic Animal Ecology.* Berlin: Springer-Verlag. 250 pp.

Ricketts, E. F., J. Calvin, and J. W. Hedgpeth (revised by D. W. Phillips). 1985. *Between Pacific Tides,* 5th ed. Stanford, CA: Stanford University Press. 652 pp.

Schell, J. 1982. *The Fate of the Earth.* New York: Knopf. 244 pp.

Slaughter, T. P. 1996. *The Natures of John and William Bartram.* New York: Knopf. 304 pp.

Slovic, S. H., and T. F. Dixon, eds. 1993. *Being in the World: An Environmental Reader for Writers.* New York: Macmillan. 726 pp.

Solnit, R. 1994. *Savage Dreams: A Journey into the Landscape Wars of the American West.* New York: Vintage. 401 pp.

Steinbeck, J. 1941. *The Log from the* Sea of Cortez. New York: Viking. 336 pp.

Sutton, G. M. 1961. *Iceland Summer.* Norman, OK: University of Oklahoma Press. 253 pp.

———. 1985. *Eskimo Year.* 2nd edition. Norman, OK: University of Oklahoma Press. 321 pp. Originally published in 1934 by Macmillan.

Terborgh, J. 1992. *Diversity and the Tropical Rain Forest.* New York: Scientific American Library (W. H. Freeman). 242 pp.

Thomas, L. 1974. *Lives of a Cell: Notes of a Biology Watcher.* New York: Viking. 153 pp.

Trefil, J. 1996. *The Edge of the Unknown: 101 Things You Don't Know About Science and No One Else Does Either.* Boston: Houghton Mifflin. 355 pp.

Vandermeer, J., I. Perfecto, and M. J. Jody. 1995. *Breakfast of Biodiversity: The Truth About Rain Forest Destruction.* Oakland California Institute for Food and Development Policy. 185 pp.

Williams, T. T. 1991. *Refuge: An Unnatural History of Family and Place.* New York: Pantheon. 304 pp.

Wilson, E. O. 1992. *The Diversity of Life.* New York: Norton. 424 pp.

———. 1994. *Naturalist.* Washington, DC: Island Press. 380 pp.

Young, L. B. 1977. *Earth's Aura.* New York: Knopf. 305 pp.

Zimmerman, J. L. 1990. *Cheyenne Bottoms: Wetland in Jeopardy.* Lawrence, KS: University of Kansas Press. 197 pp.

Zinsser, H. 1934. *Rats, Lice and History.* Boston: Atlantic/Little, Brown. 301 pp.

Zwinger, A. 1975. *Run, River, Run: A Naturalist's Journey Down One of the Great Rivers of the West.* New York: Harper & Row. 317 pp.

———. 1995. *Downcanyon: A Naturalist Explores the Colorado River Through the Grand Canyon.* Tucson, AZ: University of Arizona Press. 318 pp.

Zwinger, A., and B. E. Willard. 1972. *Land Above the Trees: A Guide to American Alpine Tundra.* New York: Harper & Row. 489 pp.